Chinese Embroidery

Wang Yarong

KODANSHA INTERNATIONAL
Tokyo and New York

Unless otherwise stated, the pictures are all furnished by the author and
the Research Group of Dress and Ornaments of the Research Institute of
History, affiliated with the Chinese Academy of Social Science.

Distributed in the United States by Kodansha International/USA Ltd.,
through Harper & Row, Publishers, Inc., 10 East 53rd Street, New York,
New York 10022. Published by Kodansha International Ltd., 2-2 Otowa
1-chome, Bunkyo-ku, Tokyo 112, and Kodansha International/ USA Ltd.,
10 East 53rd Street, New York,   New York 10022.

Copyright © 1985 and 1987 by The Commercial Press, Hong Kong Branch
First Kodansha International English Edition: 1987

Managing Editor: Chan Man Hung
Executive Editors: (Chinese Edition): Yim Lai Kuen
                   (Kodansha International English Edition):
                   Laura Cehanowicz Tringali (Chief)
                   Pun Man See

Translated by Shi Huiqing
Edited by Laura Cehanowicz Tringali

Art Co-ordination and Design: Wan Yat Sha, Yau Pik Shan
Art Editor: Wan Yat Sha
Chief Translator: Chen Tifang
Translator: Shi Huiqing

Printed and bound in Hong Kong by C & C Joint Printing Co., (H.K.)
Ltd.
This version for sale only in the United States of America and Japan.

ISBN 0-87011-825-0 (U.S.)
ISBN 4-7700-1325-0 (JAPAN)
LCC 87-45209

CONTENTS

List of Plates and Figures

4

Figures

A
BRIEF HISTORY
OF
CHINESE
EMBROIDERY

(I)

Embroidery is one of the finest Chinese arts. Popularly known as *xiuhua* or *zhahua* (繡花 or 扎花; both meaning making ornamental designs in cloth with a needle), embroidery has been used since ancient times to create works of enormous beauty and complexity. The characters *jin* (錦; brocade) and *xiu* (繡; embroidery) have been used together from time immemorial by the Chinese to describe splendid or exquisite things — as in, for instance, the phrases meaning a land of incomparable beauty (*jinxiu* land), a promising future (*jinxiu* prospects), or wit (*jin* mind, *xiu* mouth). The designs on brocade and embroidery, however, are formed quite differently: in brocade, the design is made directly on the loom by lifting warp threads (a method called *tihua*), while in embroidery, the design. is stitched on finished fabric using needles and colored silk threads.[1] Needles and thread are to a skilled embroiderer what brush, ink, and color are to a painter. Since every age boasted famous embroiderers, a considerable quantity of work must have been left behind, but because of the perishability of silk goods, only a few specimens have survived. These are now being carefully kept by collectors in China and abroad.

Throughout its long history, the art of embroidery has flourished: records of the Qin dynasty (221-206 B.C.) mention "embroidered robes and undergarments," "imperial robes and embroidered undergarments," and "white robes embroidered with red designs."[2] *Shang shu,* a history book of an earlier period, tells the story in its *Book of Yu* of how Shun, the legendary emperor, ordered Yu to make clothes: "I want to see the pictures done by the ancients: those drawn in imitation of the sun, the moon, stars, mountain, dragon, and pheasant as well as those embroidered in the forms of ritual wine vessels, aquatic plants, fire, white rice, and the designs of *fŭ* (黼) [patterns in black and white colors] and *fú* (黻) [patterns in black and blue colors]. These are to be in brilliant colors and added to dyed cloth to make garments." This was, in fact, the celebrated official costume in twelve colors used by the Son of Heaven (emperor).[3] Worn by ancient monarchs, it usually consisted of an upper garment decorated with paintings in six colors and a lower garment ornamented with embroidered designs, also in six colors. This sacred and traditional style of dress was passed from generation to generation until the end of the Qing dynasty (1644-1912). Yuan Shiai, who sought to restore the monarchy after the founding of the Republic, took great interest in reviving the use of this official costume.

Though multicolored figured brocade became popular in the Spring-and-Autumn (770-476 B.C.) and Warring States (475-221 B.C.) periods,[4] it could not compare with embroidery in artistic appeal, especially in large-scale designs. Moreover, the upper echelons of society put a premium on clothes showing either painted or embroidered designs, because of the difficult techniques involved in making them and the dictates of tradition. Precious relics excavated in recent decades illustrate that gradually the art of embroidery attained perfection. The earliest proof is in the traces of embroidered rhombic designs on a Shang (ca. 1500-1066 B.C.) bronze wine vessel,[5] and the impression of work embroidered in chain stitch found in a Western Zhou (ca. 1066-771 B.C.) tomb at Rujiazhuang, Baoji, Shanxi Province[6] (Pl. 1). Later examples are the embroidered pieces of silk found in a tomb in the state of Huang, dating from the early Spring-and-Autumn period, at Guangshan, Xinyang, Henan Province (Pl. 2); an embroidered phoenix design of Eastern Zhou unearthed in the Soviet Union;[7] and a fragment of phoenix-patterned embroidery found in a Chu tomb at Changsha, Hunan Province.[8] Particularly noteworthy are the embroidered clothes and bedding of the middle and late Warring States period (between the fourth and the third centuries B.C.), discovered in No. 1 Chu tomb at Mashan, Jiangling, Hubei Province, in early 1982[9] (Pls. 3, 4). The good condition in which these are preserved, their beautiful colors, diversity of bold and ingenious patterns, and lively, flowing artistic styles, elevate these objects far above all previous discoveries. In addition to showing a high level of technical skill, they are both ornamental and utilitarian.

Even more embroidery has survived from the two Han dynasties (206 B.C. -A.D. 220). Most typical are those found in No. 1 and No. 3 Han tombs at Mawangdui, Changsha, Hunan Province.[10] While far less splendid than those of the Warring States period, these embroideries are still beautiful and elegant (Pl. 5). Though somewhat smaller in size, the chain-stitched designs are practically indistinguishable from embroidery of the same period found in the northwest. This suggests that under the unified rule of the Qin and Han imperial governments[11] embroidery was becoming somewhat standardized. An embroidered work having a motif of tiny flowers on stems, discovered in a Western Han tomb in Jiangling (Pl. 6), may represent a design popular with the common people. Embroideries from the two Han dynasties have also been discovered in Beijing (Dabaotai),

1. Impressions of chain-stitch embroidery found in a Western Zhou tomb at Rujiazhuang, Baoji, Shanxi Province.

2. Fragment of chain-stitch embroidery found in a tomb of the state of Huang (early Spring-and-Autumn period) at Guangshan, Xinyang, Henan Province.

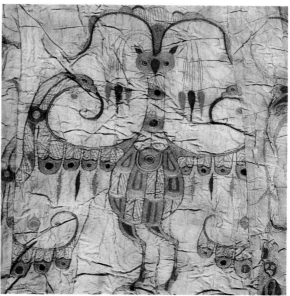

4. Bird embroidered in chain stitch, found in No. 1 Chu tomb at Mashan, Jiangling, Hubei Province (Warring States period).

3. Tiger design embroidered in chain stitch, found in No. 1 Chu tomb at Mashan, Jiangling, Hubei Province (Warring States period).

5. Chain-stitched design symbolizing longevity, found in No. 1 Han tomb at Mawangdui, Changsha, Hunan Province.

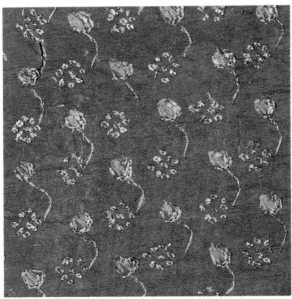

8. Appliqué work with silk and feathers, found in No. 1 Han tomb at Mawangdui, Changsha, Hunan Province.

6. Design of tiny flowers embroidered in chain stitch, found in a Western Han tomb at Fenghuangshan, Jiangling, Hubei Province.

9. Facsimile of an embroidered piece unearthed in Xinjiang (painted by Wang Xu).

7. Geometric design embroidered in single close-knit stitch, a type of satin stitch, found in No. 1 Han tomb at Mawangdui, Changsha, Hunan Province.

Gansu (Wuwei), Shanxi (Huaian), Xinjiang (Niya and Luobunaoer), and places beyond the national frontier (Pamila and Nuoyinwula). [12] They shed new light on the state of the embroidering art two thousand years ago.

Most of the examples above were worked in chain stitch, where designs are formed by linking tiny rings of colored silk thread together in chains. Whether used to embroider lines or patches, this method predominated for more than 1700 years — between the Shang dynasty and the last years of the Eastern Han dynasty. There are many varieties of chain stitch, among them loop and daisy stitches (to form dots and strokes) and consecutive stitches (used to define the thin end of a fine line). Only rarely were other techniques used, such as satin stitching, where stitches are worked so closely together that they resemble satin. Examples do exist, however, among the embroideries of Western Han (Pl. 7); some of these also use knot stitches, in which designs are made of tiny knots, and incorporate exotic materials such as silk and feathers [13] (Pl. 8). As the need grew to embroider realistic images of Buddha, human faces, lilies, peonies, and mandarin ducks, the satin stitch was used more widely. The commencement of the Jin (265-316) and Southern and Northern dynasties (420-581) saw its rapid development. Satin-stitching reached full maturity after the Sui (581-618) and Tang (618-907) dynasties, and thereafter a host of various skills blossomed. The flower-and-bird embroidered-painting style that came to maturity in the succeeding Song dynasty (960-1279) lent itself to further development of these skills.

Judging from its evolution, in its early stages embroidery was obviously meant to serve practical purposes. Adorning clothes with painted or embroidered designs might even have been a natural extension of the custom of tattooing prevalent among primitive people. Being a simpler way to create figures on fabric weaving, embroidery also required few materials at a time when resources were extremely limited, and the results were both useful and durable. In the latter respect, chain-stitching is far superior to satin-stitching, which accounts for its prevalence over so lengthy a course of history. Eventually, embroidery would be used to create objects purely for display and admiration, but the sophisticated skills necessary to achieve this took a long, long time to evolve.

Religious subjects and images of birds and flowers embroidered in winding stitches and close-knit stitches (both types of satin stitch) are commonly seen on relics of the Tang dynasty. Embroidery artists of the time also worked in another type of satin stitch, the layered short-straight stitch, using silks of related colors in graduated tones to create a shaded effect (Pl. 9). By this time, the *pingjin* method (gluing a piece of gold foil on sheepskin or paper and then cutting it into thin strips for use in embroidering) had already developed. The object described by the Tang poet Bai Juyi as being decorated with strips of gold and strings of pearls must have used this method. The embroidered works discovered in a Liao (a dynasty established by a nomadic people called Qidan) tomb, built about 960 at Yemaotai, Faku, Liaoning Province, illustrate that the skills just described continued to play a major role, with the Tang style predominating in embroidering deer and flowers; these were all done using winding stitches, supplemented by consecutive stitches and couching (overlaying a thick thread on a design, then anchoring it with fine stitches) here and there. A small scent bag adorned with silver- and gold-foil strips achieves a perfect harmony between craftsmanship and art (Pls. 10, 11).

In the latter part of the Northern Song dynasty an imperial embroidery workshop was set up in the capital — three hundred embroiderers supplied the court with products both for daily use and display. Embroidered paintings and embroidered calligraphies, produced under the influence of the academic school of painting, became popular. During the succeeding dynasties of Southern Song and Yuan (1280-1368), a new school of embroidery was formed in the south under the patronage of intellectuals who either served in the government or lived in retirement in the country. This school specialized in creating embroidered pictures and calligraphies purely for visual display. As embroidery grew ever farther from its roots in folk art, it gradually became one with painting, devoting itself to the production of artworks after the style of painters and calligraphers such as Huang Quan, Cui Bai, Su Shi, and Mi Fu. So that the embroideries would look just like the original artworks, complete with the effect of ink and brushstrokes, new techniques in stitchery and coloration had to be devised. Innovations in the art of satin stitching were thus stimulated. The Southern Song embroidered painting *Riding a Crane over a Beautiful Terrace* (Pl. 12), based on a picture by a famous artist, was made using no less than fifteen techniques, including the mixed straight stitch, darning, stem stitch, consecutive stitch, knot stitch, net stitch, pine-needle stitch, random stitch, and couching. Gold accents and colors supplemented the stitching. This work is truly representative in terms of the stitchwork used and the painterly blending of colors, but the techniques involved are actually practically the same as those used in the everyday objects unearthed from Huang Sheng's tomb (Southern Song) in Fuzhou. [14] While this confirms the high level of folk embroidery at the time, it also suggests that the skills used by the school of embroidered painting were derived from the humbler but more popular art of folk embroidery.

In addition to satin stitching, other Southern Song embroideries found in Shanxi use gauze embroidering and chuosha (both resembling petit point in the West). The strong decorative effect produced by these two methods profoundly influenced the development of some skills used in later Suzhou embroidery. Clearly, a growing repertoire of popular embroidery techniques paved the way for the technical development of a more sophisticated form of the art.

The Yuan rulers showed particular interest in embroidered works adorned with gold. Since there was a government-run embroidery factory making a variety of everyday items, much progress must have been made in the use of gold. Unfortunately, few specimens of the time have survived. However, we can still gain insight into the achievements of that dynasty through Lotus Sutra and Prajnaparamita Sutra embroideries preserved at the Liaoning Provincial Museum (Pl. 13). The latter is distinguished by the use of single threads to outline the images, in imitation of the Song painter Li Gonglin's strokes. In addition, the patterns that decorate the clothes worn by the holy personages are done with various types of net stitchery (pattern embroidery), which by then had been established as an independent embroidery form.

Inspired by the work of Song and Yuan artists, the Gu family, living at Luxiangyuan, Jiangsu Province, in the last years of the Ming dynasty (1368-1644), specialized in embroidering reproductions of pictures done by famous artists. They became leaders of fashion and taste, and though often credited with more than they achieved, they did succeed in advancing the skills of the Song and Yuan dynasties. But the Maitreya they embroidered, shown sitting on a hassock made of cattails and wearing a robe adorned with extremely complex designs, seems to have gone too far in its effort to imitate reality. However, the Gu family did create a new type of stitching technique. Inspired by the painter You Qiu's use of extremely fine lines to outline human figures, they developed "hair embroidery," [15] in which the hair of newborn babies was incorporated into the design.

This kind of embroidery made little impression on common folk, who needed embroideries that were practical as well as ornamental. Satin stitching, however, which was developed by sophisticated embroidery artists, was embraced by folk embroiderers and did much to expand their already rich repertoire of skills.

In the early stages of the Qing dynasty, with the revival of the national economy, a handcrafted textile industry engaged in the production of embroidered household articles began to thrive on the foundation established during the Ming dynasty. As embroidering techniques kept improving and the dress of the upper classes became more and more luxurious, for a time the costly method of split-color-floss embroidering was universally adopted. Commercial houses, which went by the name of "Gu's embroidery shop," were set up in the cities — they took orders and sold all sorts of objects including embroidered theatrical costumes and embroideries for or-namentation, gift-giving, daily use, and export. But as the demand for everyday embroideries increased, more and more families began to produce them, and local products could be found competing in marketplaces all over the country. The most famous of these were made in Suzhou, Guangdong, Sichuan, and Hunan. Ranking next were those made in Beijing, Shanghai, Shandong, Hangzhou, Wenzhou, Fujian, and Kaifeng. Embroideries were also produced by minority peoples in northwest and southwest China, including the Miao, the Mongolians, the Uigurs, the Yi, the Li, and the Hani who, with their different backgrounds and traditions, produced a great variety of exquisite, unique, and useful works.

Many and varied are the techniques involved in embroidery, and it is virtually impossible to represent every one of them here. Consequently, only the most important stitches are discussed in this book. Embroidery had become a universal pastime for women, who practiced it all their lives. As a result, "even the dullest ones became expert, and practice made perfect." The ensuing period saw the full flowering of the art and a stunning array of techniques and products.

(II)

The plates in this book chiefly show small, wearable embroidered ornaments made after the seventeenth century. They include collars, cuffs, bags of various shapes and sizes (including scent bags, fan cases, spectacle cases, mirror cases, key cases, and scissors cases), pin cushions, and pouches for tailor's chalk. There are also a few samples of embroideries made by minority groups. Besides

10. Embroidered scent bag found in a Liao tomb at Yemaotai, Liaoning Province.

12. Embroidered painting, *Riding a Crane over a Beautiful Terrace,* Southern Song dynasty (preserved at the Liaoning Provincial Museum).

11. Detail of an embroidered cap found in a Liao tomb at Yemaotai, Liaoning Province.

13. Embroidered Buddhist painting with the image of Buddha worked in net stitch, Yuan dynasty (preserved at the Liaoning Provincial Museum).

14. Facsimile of a Tang embroidered scent bag with a design symbolizing good luck and success, unearthed in Xinjiang (painted by Wang Xu).

those made for sale by the artisans of the bag shops, most of the embroideries were worked by women in their homes for ornamentation. They differ greatly in style, depending on when and where they were made and the background of the embroiderer.

The embroidered objects meant to be hung at the waist, [16] such as scent bags, pouches, and fan cases, merit particular attention because they were used by all people, regardless of age, sex, rank, or race. They were therefore among the most typical accessories made by folk embroiderers. The custom of wearing bags to hold various things or fragrant leaves began as early as the Shang and Zhou dynasties. Among the funerary objects discovered in tombs of the time were pin cases and knives worn at the waist. The earliest written record of this custom can be found in the *Book of Rites, (Li ji),* a book of the Han dynasty. The section on domestic conduct relates that in the days of Qin, men wore leather *pan* and women wore silk *pan.* These were later described by Zheng Xuan of the Eastern Han dynasty as small bags, usually painstakingly decorated, to hold towels. The book also names a dozen or so objects that a son was obliged to carry to serve his parents; including towels, knives, whetstones, awls for undoing knots, and fire-making tools. Likewise, a wife was required to carry a bag of sewing implements to serve her husband's parents. Young people of both sexes who had not come of age wore scent bags to show respect for their seniors. [17] (Rigid rules governed the way all these bags were worn.) Since they were carried constantly, no effort was spared to have these bags finely crafted.

The relics found in the Han tomb at Mawangdui show that the scent bag of the time was rather large and consisted of a body, a top, a bottom, a neck, and a drawstring. They were usually made of high-quality silk and, when filled with aromatic plant leaves, [18] could be used as sachet or carried about. But if we compare this type of bag with the scent bags described in the famous Han poem *The Peacock Flying to the Southeast,* which were attached to the four corners of a mosquito net, we can see that it could not be used as a hanging ornament. Instead it might resemble the early Tang scent bag unearthed in Xinjiang (Pl. 14). An Eastern Han record also describes an "embroidered bag with the design of tiger head" worn on one side of the waist. Called a side bag or ribbon bag, it contained the ribbon attached to the official seal. Just such a bag is depicted in a stone carving discovered in a Han tomb at Yinan, Shandong Province [19] (Pl. 15); clearly, the embroidery is worked in chain stitch. In the *History of the Three Kingdoms (San guo zhi),* Cao Cao, the founder of the Wei dynasty (220-265), was described as "dressed in light silk and wearing a small bag to hold towels and sundry things." Early in the Tang dynasty it became a rule that all people carry on their bodies seven objects, [20] similar to those carried by people in ancient times. In the Song, Yuan, Liao, and Jin dynasties, the nomadic peoples of the north customarily wore a bag containing a flint, knife, and whetstone (Pl. 16).

During the Qing dynasty (1644-1911), waist-hung embroidered bags were much in vogue (Pl. 17). (A complete set of these was popularly called "court-style nine objects.") This fashion was perpetuated by the ruling groups — the Manchurians and the Mongolians — who clung to their old customs despite being at the top of the social scale. Fancily embroidered dress and ornaments were used by members of the nobility to display their wealth, and decorative embroidered objects were given as presents by the court as well as by officials among themselves. In fact, these items became indispensable to social interaction. The prevailing sense of peace and order throughout the land, and the development of a handcrafted-textile industry, encouraged these practices. To take the example of scent bags, the *Gu wan zhi nan xubian (Sequel to a Guide to Collectors of Antiques)* says: "People in all walks of life — rich or poor, of noble or common birth — wore scentbags in summer. They were obtainable in every corner of the capital city. Even more numerous were the bags offered for sale at the fair and marketplace (Pl. 18). In those days, a man would be thought untidily dressed if he failed to carry a scent bag on a hot day, thus causing pain to himself and drawing the censure of the public. People attached so much importance to them that even the lower strata spared no pains to procure them. Every skill used in embroidery was employed to embellish the object so much sought after, and the rich took pride in the extremely fine fancy works in their possession." The bags took different forms, but in the city the most popular shapes were the chicken heart, ellipse, and gourd. Two verses from poems written in the middle and late periods of the Qing dynasty satirize the abuses of the times, using the small embroidered bags as examples. The first is from *Poem After the Bamboo Twig Pattern* (one of the set patterns in Chinese poetry) composed by Yang Miren (taken from the 1796 edition):

Suishang piao makes finest pipes,
Zierbenzhi made of fine jade.
Knotting and use of gold accent are all the go,
And the Hui [Uigur] bags tied with silk threads. [21]

The next example is from De Shuoting's poem *A String of Rough Pearls* (written during the reign of Jiaqing, 1796-1820):

> Knotting, *pingjin,* and appliqué
> are not much to brag about,
> Just see how many womenfolk
> spend their time on *chuosha.*

There are innumerable such verses, and from them we learn that not only the fashions, but the skills of the times were ever changing. The knot stitch and the use of gold accent, for example, were popular in the last years of Qianlong (around 1795), but during the reign of Jiaqing (1796-1820), *chuosha* (a type of weave-in embroidery) gained public favour. Later on, however, the techniques of *dazi* (knotting) and *pingjin* (filling with gold) were preferred. The poems also tell us that these fine works of art were primarily made by women of humbler families.

In the cities, women used very small bags, which were usually exquisitely made. A woman might wear one or two scent bags, a silver earpick, silver tweezers, and the like — "three silver things" or "seven silver things." Aristocratic women often wore bags made of gold and jewels to display their wealth (Pl. 19). With the exception of a negligible quantity sold to commercial houses, these elaborate small embroideries, made by folk embroiderers, were not for sale. Instead they were given as gifts on occasions such as weddings and festivals. Sometimes articles such as miniature umbrellas, fans, clothes, and shoes of extremely fine workmanship were dedicated to the gods.

In the early decades of this century, girls in the rural areas of North China began to practice needlework and embroidery at the age of six or seven. Upon reaching marriageable age, each girl was required to prepare a considerable number of tiny embroidered bags, not only in the common shapes of the chicken heart, gourd, and ellipse, but in the form of flower baskets, lotus seedpods, silver ingots, lanterns, double fish, double coins and *zong* (resembling a quadrilateral pyramid) wound with colored threads. All these are auspicious motifs, and they were further adorned with hanging loops, decorative knots, or tassels made of colored silk. When they were completed, the tiny bags were strung together and put into colored-straw baskets woven in the shape of flowers or fruit; the beginning of the string of bags was attached to the cover of the basket. On the day of the wedding, when friends and relatives crowded in to have a look at the dowry of the bride, the strings of beautifully made bags would be ample evidence of her skill and cleverness. The bride would then present these bags to her elder female relatives such as her mother-in-law, and elderly friends, as well as to her new sisters-in-law. Also in anticipation of the marriages, usually twelve pairs (in the case of rich families, one hundred pairs) of embroidered shoes were made. As both the Chinese characters for "shoe" and "together" are pronounced *xie,* this gift symbolized that the newly married couple would live together to a great age. The ornamental collar, which evolved from the "robe of feathers" of the Sui dynasty, was fashionable among both men and women of the nobility during the Yuan dynasty. It was made by joining together heartlike S-shapes (*ruyi* motif; Pls. 81-85)[22]; this pattern also influenced the decoration of porcelain vases of later periods. In the Qing dynasty, the collar was worn by all people, but especially young women. It generally had two layers made of eight parts, each embroidered

15. Stone carving found in a Han tomb at Yinan, Shandong Province, depicting a military man wearing a bag embroidered with a tiger head.

16. A Yuan tomb mural found in Chifeng, Inner Mongolia, depicting a man wearing a bag at his hip.

17. Painting entitled *The Empress Dowager Playing Chess,* showing people wearing bags and a thumb ring, Qing dynasty.

18. Painting, showing a bag peddler in Guangdong, late Qing dynasty.

19. Bags embroidered with pearls worn on the chest by women of rank, unearthed from the tomb of an imperial princess at Chifeng.

with pictures based on popular plays or designs of flowers and insects. These elaborate collars could take six to twelve months to make, and young women did their best to outdo each other in complexity. Brides worked especially hard on their collars, for they were obliged to call on their relations during the first lunar New Year after marriage wearing finery made with their own hands. This spirit of competition fostered mutual learning and embroidery that was full of originality and life. It could be matched neither by commercially made embroideries nor those that slavishly imitated the works of painters or calligraphers.

(III)

Though embroidery and brocade had been regarded as parallel arts since ancient times, embroidery really enjoyed a number of advantages. For example, being free from the restrictions imposed by the loom, embroidery was able to incorporate a wide range of themes and a great variety of designs, and to express them with personality and, perhaps more importantly, in complicated color schemes. The miscellaneous embroidered bags just discussed, though small in size, include images such as landscapes, trees, flowers, the sun, the moon, clouds, gardens, animals, insects, characters from famous stories, geometric patterns, and auspicious symbols — in fact, almost everything under the sun. Through its well-conceived compositions, varied stitching techniques, and skillful use of color, embroidery influenced artistic expression in weaving. The pile-loop brocade (*rongguan-jin*) of Western Han, for instance, was clearly imitative of a variation of chain embroidery called the loop stitch. [23] In addition, the technique of "shading" in weaving most probably originated in an attempt to duplicate the painterly feeling of color wash created through embroidering with satin stitches. Shading might have been adopted by weavers before the Sui and Tang dynasties, and influence on later ages is proven by such works as the *Yunjian* Brocade of the Tang dynasty and the *Babaozhao* Brocade and the *Badayun* Brocade of the Song dynasty, as well as by the use of wash in colored wall paintings of the Song and Ming dynasties. [24] Patterned brocade (*zhuanghua*) of the Ming dynasty might have been fashioned after the then popular skill of *chuosha* embroidery. Using a process called *kesi,* colored weft threads, each on a separate bobbin, were woven to form designs that looked as beautiful as those that were embroidered; the warp ground color was extremely harmonious and clear.

The colors used in folk embroidery are chosen either to harmonize or to contrast. Generally, items used on happy occasions, such as New Year celebrations, weddings, and birthdays are embroidered in rich, strongly contrasting colors. Items for ordinary use are usually worked in light, soft, and subtle colors, sometimes so subtle that their very quietness impresses. The embroideries of the south are finely worked, prettily colored, and full of vitality; those of the north are crude, solemnly colored, and have simple, regular patterns. The artists of Guangdong, a seaside province, have a style all their own, preferring a warm, bold color scheme uninhibited by tradition. The migrating populations who inhabit the extensive and dreary grasslands and deserts of the northwest use vivid colors to offset the dulness of the environment as well as to complement its

vastness — coloration that would be almost unbearable to a city dweller living in cramped quarters. (Similarly, the costumes of the Peking opera are embroidered in rich colors so the patterns will be visible from a distance.) Since the development of modern industry causes hand-made products to gradually drop out of everyday life, many people mistakenly believe that folk embroiderers use only loud colors. In fact, the chromatic schemes are actually extremely extensive. The records of Song, Yuan, and later ages [25] mention a great variety of colors, and it is said that in the late Qing period, several hundred different colors were produced by dyers throughout the country, including no less than thirty shades of brown. *Xue huan xiu pu,* a book devoted to the art of embroidery, relates that eighty-eight colors were used, with a total of 745 different shades. A tiny piece of embroidery is usually executed in ten or more colors.

Designs that are polychromatic can be vivid and glorious, but those using monochromatic threads can be manipulated to create the effect of shade, resulting in work that is calm and elegant. No matter what color is selected — crimson, deep blue, or black on a white ground; white on a blue ground; white, blue, or black on a scarlet ground; white or red on a green ground — the outcome can be either serene or sumptuous, depending on the design and whether it is simple or complicated, densely or thinly distributed. [26] Embroidering shiny patterns on a deep, darkish (sometimes a fresh green) ground can create a striking effect.

With small embroideries, tiny designs faintly touched with color are usually worked on a light-colored ground; large designs in rich colors are worked on a deeply colored ground. But this is by no means a hard and fast

rule. Adding borders to the designs, leaving narrow spaces between them (called voiding), and accenting with gold or silver are all employed to soften strong contrasts in color. Folk embroiderers also use graduated tones of the same color or related colors, or shading, to achieve harmony. A wide variety of color-blending skills was practiced in traditional Chinese weaving and embroidery, and color-blending formulas datable to the Ming and Qing periods were used by weavers of patterned brocade. [27] The formulas specify the "blending of two colors" and the "blending of three colors," as follows:

Blending of two colors:
>jade white and blue
>feather grey and blue
>sunflower yellow and green
>ancient bronze and purple
>crimson and pink

Blending of three colors:
>cerise, pale rose, and deep red
>azurite jade white, pale blue, and sapphire blue *giuxiang* (greenish yellow), bronze and snuff
>silvery grey, tile grey, and pigeon grey deep and light bronzes and camel date dark brown, grape, and bronze

These formulas do not include all combinations and are subject to alteration. Unfortunately, a more complete knowledge of the techniques involved does not exits.

Records of color-blending in folk embroidery can also be found in Ming and Qing novels such as *Jin ping mei* and *The Dream of the Red Chamber.* Chapter 35 of *The Dream of the Red Chamber* tells how a maid made a net for her young master Baoyu; it includes a discussion of the blending of colors.

Because dyers of the past used only natural plant dyes, the old embroideries still retain their rich, mellow, brilliant, and elegant colors. Compare the history of natural dyes, which extends over several thousand years, to that of synthesized organic dyes,[28] which were invented by W. H. Perkin in 1856. We clearly have much to learn from ancient techniques about the matching, contrasting, and mixing of colors as well as about the handling of the overall effect.

The design, workmanship, and coloration of a good piece of embroidery usually embody the wisdom, work, and feelings of generations of women. The embroiderers of the past have indeed accumulated much experience and knowledge, and when we view the results of their labors, we cannot help but feel awed. Embroideries worked in simple chromatic schemes do not appear monotonous at all, while the multicolored ones are precise and neat. The great diversity of skills and colors used are all regulated by traditional rules and help to shape a style that is robust, cheerful, charming, and splendid.

Notes

1. Xia Nai, *Archaeology and History of Science and Technology* (Beijing: Ke Xue Publishing House, 1979); p. 86.
2. These examples are found in the following parts of the *Book of Songs: Qin Folksong—Zhongnan Bin Folksong—jiuyu* (net made of rope) and *Tang Folksong — Small Creek*. For reference to embroidering with threads dyed red, see Wang Xu's "The Designs on Silk Fabrics Unearthed in a Han Tomb at Mawangdui," *Archaeological Researches,* 1979, No. 5, p. 447.
3. According to *Tong Dian,* by Du You, every design had significance: the sun, moon, and stars stood for the shedding of light; the mountain for heaviness; the dragon for change; the pheasant for beautiful designs; ancestral wine vessels for filial piety; water plants for purity; fire for brightness; rice for nourishment; the design of *fu* (in the shape of an ax) for sharpness; the design of *fu* (in the shape of the characters *yi* or *gong* arranged back to back) for distinctiveness.
4. Xiong Chuanxing, "Silk Fabrics of the Warring States Period Recently Found in Changsha," *Cultural Relics,* 1975, No. 2. Chen Yuejun and Zhan Xuqiu, "Silk Fabrics of the Warring States Period Unearthed from No. 1 Chu Tomb at Mazhuan, Jiangling," *Cultural Relics,* 1982. No. 10.
5. Vivi Sylwan, "Silk from the Yin Dynasty," *The Museum of Far Eastern Antiquities,* Stockholm, Bulletin No. 9, pp. 123-124.
6. Li Yezhen et al., "An Important Discovery Concerning the Silk Weaving and Embroidery of the Western Zhou," *Cultural Relics,* 1976, No. 4, plate I.
7. Commission for the Preservation of Historical Relics of Xinyang District, Henan Province, and the Cultural Center of Guangshan Country, "Report on the Excavation of the Tomb of Huang Junmeng and His Wife, Who Lived in Early Spring-and-Autumn Period," *Archaeological Researches,* 1984, No. 4, plate I: No. 2; Fig. 32.
8. Gao Zhixi, "A Report of the Result of a Check-up on the Contents of *Muguo* [wooden outer coffin] Tomb No. 3 at Martyrs Park, Changsha," *Cultural Relics,* 1959, No. 10, Figs. 16, 17.
9. Museum of Jingzhou District, "The Numerous Silk Fabrics of the Warring States Period Unearthed from Tomb No. 1 at Mawang Brick Factory, Jiangling County, Hubei Province," *Cultural Relics,* 1982, No. 10, upper and lower color plates. Plate II: No. 2-4; plate IV: lower and upper parts. *Jianghan Archaeological Researches,* 1982, No. 1, plate II.
10. *Han Tomb No. 1 at Mawangdui, Changsha,* final volume (Beijing; Cultural Relics Publishing House, 1973), color plates.
11. Archaeological Research Institute of the Chinese Academy of Social Science, *Report on the Excavation of a Han Tomb at Mancheng,* volume 1 (Beijing: Cultural Relics Publishing House, 1980), pp. 308-311.
12. Xia Nai, *Archaeology and History of Science and Technology* (Beijing: Ke Xue Publishing House, 1979), p. 87 and notes.
13. Two of the more reliable examples are found in E. Ljubo-Lesnichenko, *Ancient Chinese Silks and Silk Embroidery,* 1961, tables, and *Han Tomb No. 1 at Mawangdui, Changsha,* final volume (Beijing: Cultural Relics Publishing House, 1973), illustration 115.
14. Museum of Fujian Province, *Tomb of Huang Sheng of the Southern Song Dynasty Discovered in Fuzhou,* (Beijing: Cultural Relics Publishing House, 1982), pp. 128-133.
15. Shen Congwen "On Guangdong Embroidery," *Yangcheng Evening News,* August 9, 1962.
16. *A General Account of the Cultural Relics and Miscellaneous Articles of the Old Capital* (published by the Beijing branch of the China Travel Service in 1935) has it: " 'The Official Nine' and 'embroideries with gold accents' sold by the bag makers in the Qing dynasty were of all kinds and they were famous throughout the country." The "official nine" consists of a long rectangular bag with an opening in the middle (*dalian* bag), a box for visiting cards, a spectacles case, a fan case, a watch case, two scent bags, a thumb ring box, and a tobacco pouch.
17. The section on domestic conduct of the *Book of Rites (Li ji).* says: "In order to serve his parents, a son...must wear on his left side towels, a knife, a whetstone, a small awl, a piece of metal for producing sparks; and he must wear on his right side a piece of jade, a sleeve cover, a sheath, a big awl, and a piece of wood for producing fire....To serve her

husband's parents, a woman... must wear on her left side towels, knife, a whetstone, a small awl, and a piece of metal to produce fire, and she must carry on her right side needles, keys, thread, a certain quantity of cotton fiber, a bag stitched with needle and thread, a big awl, and a piece of wood for producing fire....Youths of both sexes, not old enough to wear hats or hairpins, are required to wash hands and rinse the mouth at the first crow of the cock; then comb their hair and wear scent bags on their hair knots and the lapels of their robes."

18. *Cultural Relics,* 1962, Nos. 7-8 (combined issue), color plates on p. 3.

19. *Report on the Excavation of an Ancient Tomb with Murals at Yinan,* (Board of Cultural Relics of the Ministry of Culture, 1956), plate 56, upper right, showing a figure wearing at the waist a bag embroidered with a tiger head.

20. In its part dealing with carriages and dress, the *New History of Tang* says: "In the reign of Emperor Ruizong, knives and whetstones were no longer worn. But military officers above the fifth grade still had to carry on the waist-belt seven articles, namely, a sword, a knife, a whetstone, a needlecase, a flint, etc." Relevant illustrations can be found in *A Study of the Ancient Chinese Costumes,* by Shen Congwen, published in Hong Kong by the Commercial Press, 1981. In illustration 96 on p. 254, a Gaochang mural made during the Five Dynasties is shown. It represents Uigur noblemen wearing ornamental waist belts visiting a temple. Figs. 74-76 show ladies'

costumes of the Tang dynasty with matching waist belts.

21. *Suishang piao,* a fashionable plaything of the time, was a snuff bottle with extremely thin walls carved from a piece of jade. It was so named because it would not sink when placed on water. *Zierbenzhi* is the thumb ring made out of pebblelike jade produced in Hetian, Xinjiang. One piece could cost as much as 800 tales of silver. Knotting and the use of gold accent were the prevalent skills used in embroidering small ornamental bags.

22. *Ruyi* (如意). This object was originally a kind of backscratcher. In Chinese *ruyi* means "as one wishes," and this name was given to the object because with its help one can scratch one's back with ease. Its head is reminiscent of the shape of a kind of fungus or of clouds or a heart, and its handle has an S curve.

The coiled, heartlike *ruyi* patterns shown in plates 80-85 are based on the *ruyi* instrument. Since the name has auspicious meaning, the *ruyi* motif is used on ornaments and gifts. And due to their felicitous association, *ruyi* designs are very popular with the Chinese.

23. *Report on the Excavation of a Han Tomb at Mancheng,* volume 1 (Beijing: Cultural Relics Publishing House, 1980), p. 159; *Han Tomb No. 1 at Mawangdui, Changsha,* final volume (Cultural Relics Publishing House, 1973), illustration 137.

24. Shen Congwen *The Art of Making Dragon and Phoenix Designs: Brocade Adorned with Gold* (Writers' Publishing House, 1960), p. 4.

25. Refer to the following books: *Suijin* ("A Collection of Gems"), a photoprint edition made in 1935 by the Palace Museum, Beijing. Song Yingxing (Ming), *Tiangong kaiwu* ("Things Made by Heaven and Hand"),(Guangdong People's Publishing House, 1976). *Moe xiaolu* ("Scriber's Notes"), a blockprint edition published by Juhao Hall of the Wu family in the fifth year of Longqing of Mi. A photoprint edition of this was published by the China Book Store in 1959.

Li Dou (Qing), *Reminiscences of Yangzhou* (Zhonghua Book Co.). Chu Hua, *Mumian pu* ("Register of Cotton Fabrics"), one of a series of books entitled *Historical Anecdotes of Shanghai,* published in 1935.

The names of the colors in different shades that appear in the above-mentioned books are grouped together. (These names, given by users who lived in different historical periods, were by no means standardized. The same tint might have several names, whose exact meanings are often unintelligible to even professional embroiderers.)

(1) Red and purple — deep red, light red, cardinal red, red of the south, vermilion, cinnabar, persimmon, peach, lotus seed, plum, date, wood red, pale pink, pale rose, pink, crimson, flesh color, rouge, dark red, "near" red, coral, faded red, Huaian red, never-old red, *boluo* (name of a plant) red, fallen-leaf red,

pomegranate, apricot pink, *lu*-peach red, real purple, deep purple, rose purple, aubergine, heliotrope, cockscomb.

(2) *Qing*. In Chinese this character means both blue and green — dark blue, reddish blue, golden blue, deep blue, indigo blue, blue-and-green, prime minister's blue (the Song dynasty prime minister Cai Jing wore blue robes), Buddha-head blue, Gaiyang blue, grape blue, *he* blue, *tian* blue (deep blue with a reddish tint), azurite, *fen* (powder) blue, prawn blue, crab blue, egg blue, blue of the first degree, blue of the second degree, blue of the third degree, sapphire blue, greenish blue, sky blue, sea blue, Chaozhou blue, Suining blue, *guyue* (old moon) color, feather grey, jade white, *yuexiabai* (below-the-moon white), official green, *guang* green, pea green, bud green, glossy dark green, dark green, willow green, wheat green, lake green (light green), bamboo-stalk green, onion-root green, cypress-branch green, duckhead green, parrot green, grape green, *pingpo* (name of a fruit) green.

(3) Yellow and ochre — golden yellow, bright yellow, cardinal yellow, fresh yellow, gardenia yellow, persimmon yellow, willow yellow, ginger yellow, locust-tree yellow, sunflower yellow, light yellow camel-wool color, reddish yellow, ochre, honey yellow, apricot yellow, corn yellow.

(4) Black and white — black, sweet black, raw black, mature black, glossy inky dark, *buke* black, moon white, grass white, bleached white, ivory white.

(5) Light and deep brown — reddish brown, dark brown, dry ash color, reddish black, snuff, bronze, chestnut, wool color, *lu* (reed) dark brown, date dark brown, Jing dark brown, ink dark brown, tea brown, *jie* (dark brown)-tea brown, green-tea brown, gharu-wood brown, lilac brown, rat brown, musk brown, eagle-back brown, pigeon-neck brown, brick brown, silvery brown, felt brown, camel brown, lotus-root brown, grape brown, onion-white brown, pea-green brown, chaste-tree brown, mugwort brown, frost brown, dew brown, birchleaf-pear brown, oil chestnut brown, sandalwood brown, dry bamboo brown, mountain brown, lake water brown, pearl brown, lotus seed brown.

(6) Gold and silver—gold decoration, *lujin* (gold thread), colors intermingled with gold, *giangjin* (sprinkled with gold), gold edging, *jiejin,* carved gold, twisted gold, sunken gold, bright gold, gold dust, *bangjin,* gold-back, *yinjin* (gold-shadow), *lanjin* (gold barrier), *panjin* (filling with gold thread), gold knitting, gold thread, fastening of gold foil, *pingjin* thread (gold-wrapped thread), gold and silver serrated edge, gold and silver background.

26. Deng Yu, "Sichuan's *tiaohua* embroidery," *Decoration*, 1959, No. 3.
27. Yan Ming, "Traditional Techniques Used in Making Yunnan Brocade."
28. The purple dye invented by W. H. Perkin in 1856 was at first called aniline purple. It was later renamed mauveine and was soon introduced into China. It is the very color called *yanlianzi* (imported lotus purple), used in Chinese embroidery and noted for its superficial showiness and lack of quiet simplicity.

EMBROIDERED
OBJECTS

Accessories

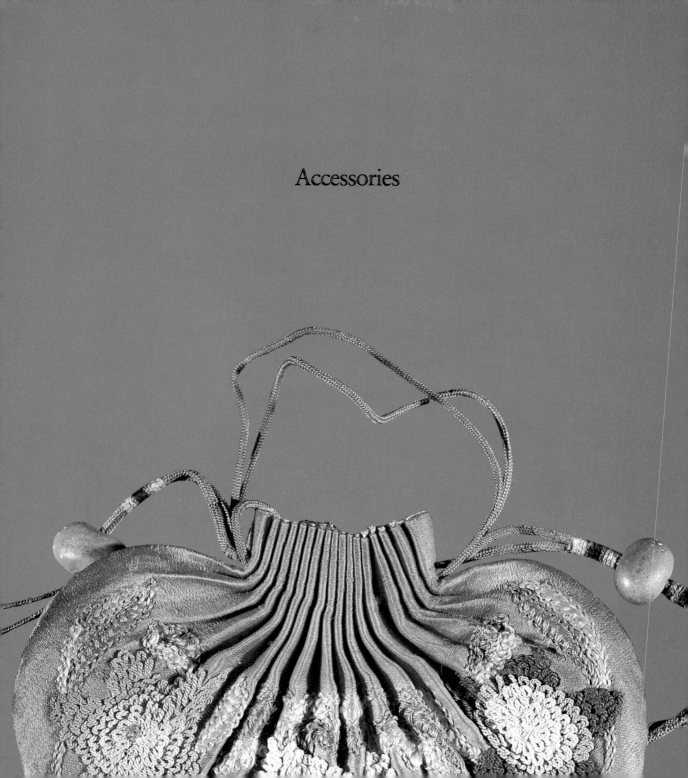

20. Oval bag worn at the waist with a design of a *qilin* (a mythical animal) carrying a child, embroidered in knot stitch, eyebrow and eyelash stitch, and couching with palm fibers.

21. Oval bag worn at the waist with motifs symbolizing happiness, wealth, and longevity, embroidered in knot stitch and couching with palm fibers.

22. Oval bag worn at the waist with design of three crabs, embroidered in knot stitch and couched.

23. Oval bag worn at the waist with "from all corners of the land" design.

24. Oval bag worn at the waist with tiger design.

25. Scent bag with designs of plum, orchid, chrysanthemum, and bamboo, embroidered with the type of weave-in embroidery called *chuosha*.

26. Scent bag with flower designs and the double-happiness character *(xi)*, embroidered in knot stitch.

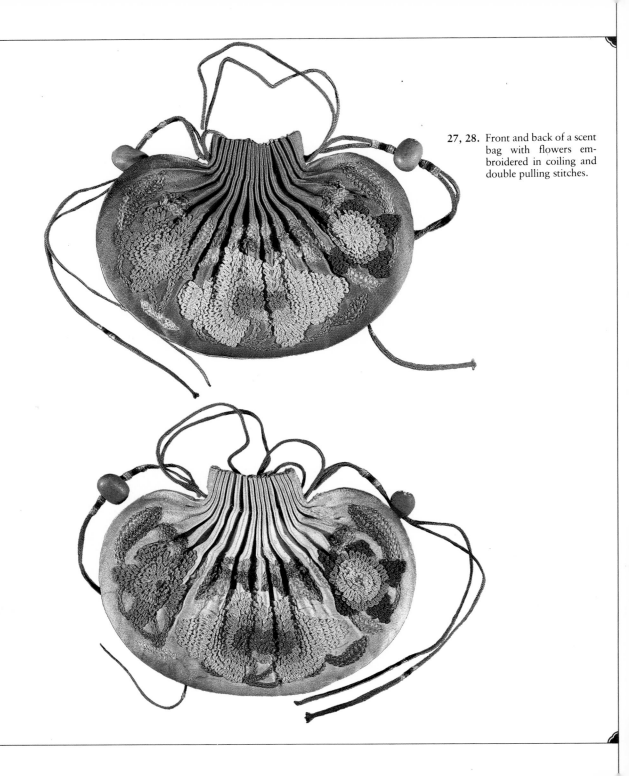

27, 28. Front and back of a scent bag with flowers embroidered in coiling and double pulling stitches.

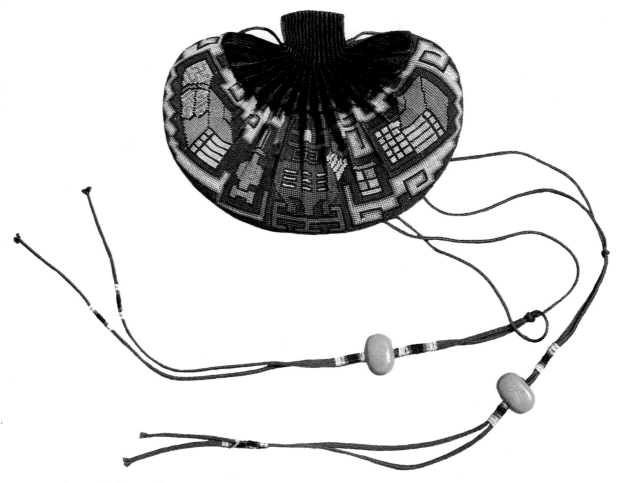

29. Scent bag with design of ancient objects, gauze-embroidering.

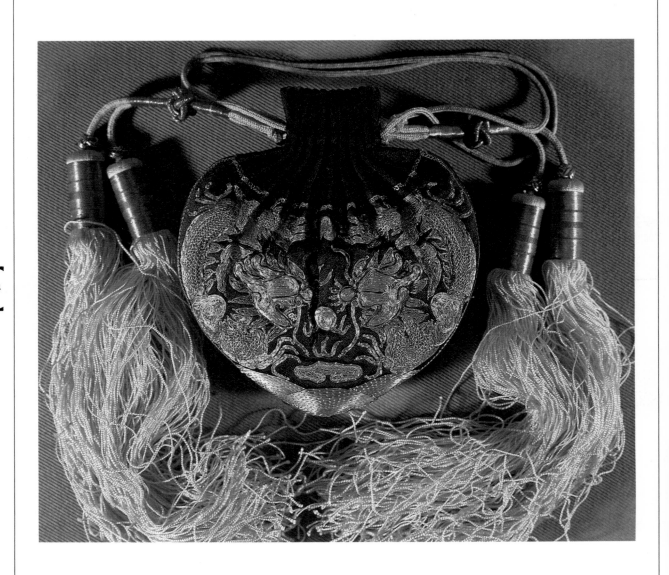

30. Heart-shaped scent bag with "two dragons playing with a pearl" design, couching with gold and silver thread, pulling stitch, and knot stitch.

31. Heart-shaped scent bag with deer and cranes design.

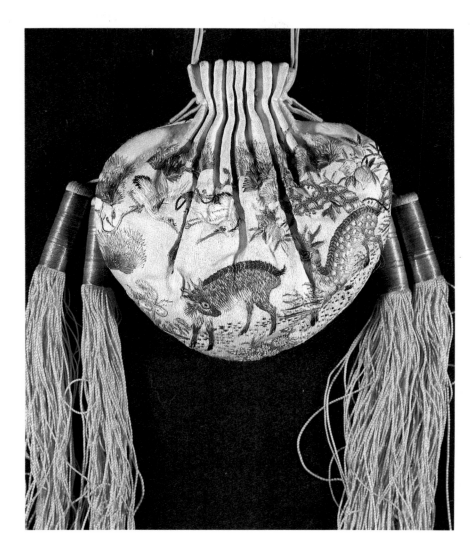

32. Gourd-shaped tobacco pouch with butterfly and melons design, embroidered in knot stitch.

33. Gourd-shaped bag with bat, child, and fish designs, chiefly embroidered in satin stitch.

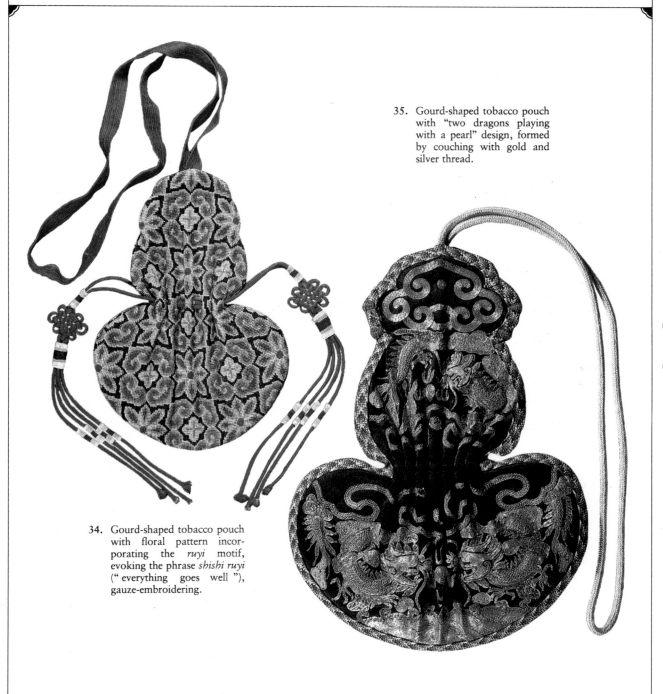

35. Gourd-shaped tobacco pouch with "two dragons playing with a pearl" design, formed by couching with gold and silver thread.

34. Gourd-shaped tobacco pouch with floral pattern incorporating the *ruyi* motif, evoking the phrase *shishi ruyi* (" everything goes well "), gauze-embroidering.

36. *Dalian* (bag sewn at both ends with an opening in the middle, usually worn at the waist), with designs symbolizing many children and longevity, made by circling with gold thread, winding stitch, and darning embroidery.

37. *Dalian* bag with designs symbolizing longevity, gauze-embroidering.

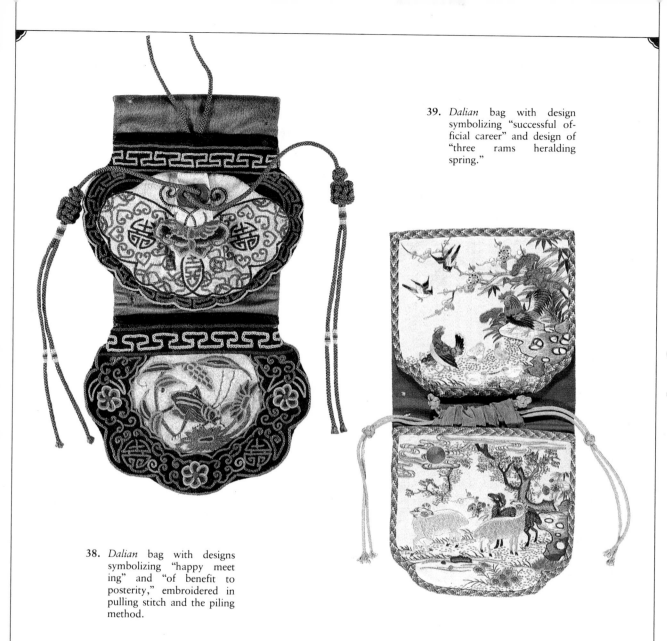

39. *Dalian* bag with design symbolizing "successful official career" and design of "three rams heralding spring."

38. *Dalian* bag with designs symbolizing "happy meeting" and "of benefit to posterity," embroidered in pulling stitch and the piling method.

40, 41. Square bags with human figures representing characters in traditional plays, embroidered in knot and satin stitches and couching with palm fibers.

42. Square bag with designs symbolizing wealth, embroidered in pulling stitch, consecutive stitch, knot stitch, eyebrow and eyelash stitch, fastening stitch, and pine-needle stitch.

43. Square bag with "dragon playing with phoenix" design, embroidered in knot stitch, scattering stitch, consecutive stitch, piling method and couching.

44. Square bag with melons design, embroidered in knot stitch, winding stitch, pulling stitch, and couching.

45. Square bag with design of blue flowers, embroidered primarily in flat stitchwork.

43

46. Bag with designs symbolizing "first on the list of successful candidates in the Civil Service examination for three times" and "entertaining great expectations for one's son," embroidered with a variety of techniques.

47. Bag embroidered with double threads. The main stitches used are single close-knit stitch, fastening stitch, stem stitch, winding stitch, and slanting satin stitch.

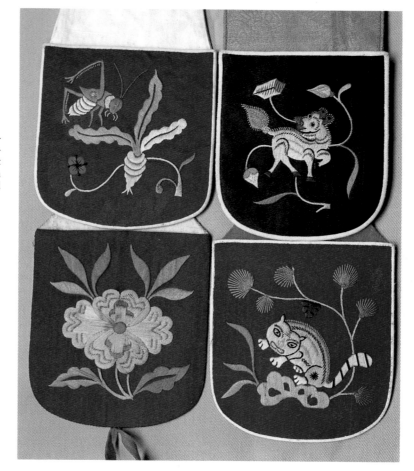

48. Pouch, embroidered with couching and pulling, knot, and net stitches.

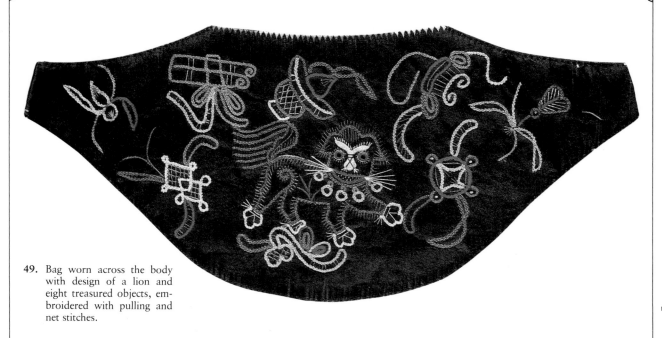

49. Bag worn across the body with design of a lion and eight treasured objects, embroidered with pulling and net stitches.

50. Bag worn across the body with "two phoenixes playing with a peony" design.

51. Bag for handkerchiefs with pattern of a bird with a flower in its beak, gauze-embroidering.

52. Bag for handkerchiefs with "two dragons competing for a treasure" design, couching with palm fibers.

53. Bag for handkerchiefs with pattern of Chinese character for longevity (*shou*) and felicitous motifs, couching with palm fibers.

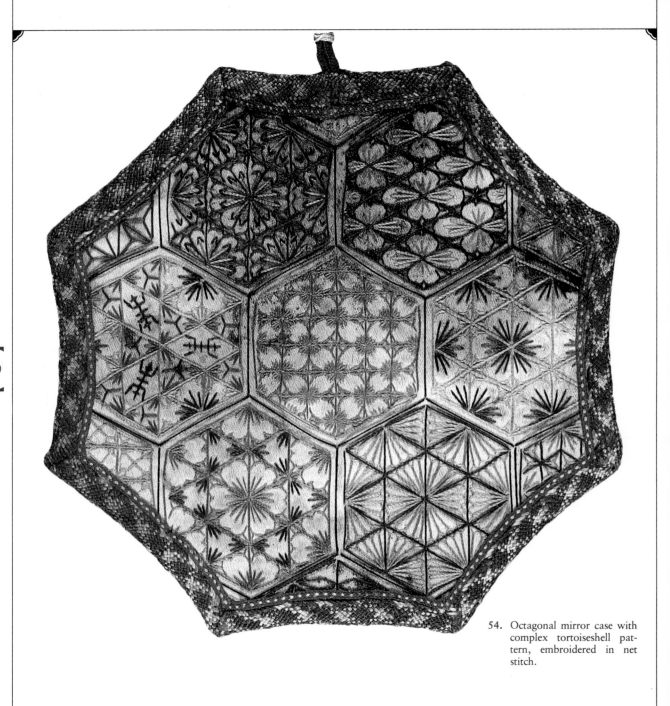

54. Octagonal mirror case with complex tortoiseshell pattern, embroidered in net stitch.

55. Round mirror case with pattern of human figures, birds, and geometric forms, gauze-embroidering.

56, 57. Front and back of a fan case with designs of vegetables and insects, couching with palm fibers.

58. Fan case with design of ancient objects, couching with gold and silver thread and several other techniques.

59. Toy case with "two dragons playing with a pearl" design, couching with gold and silver thread.

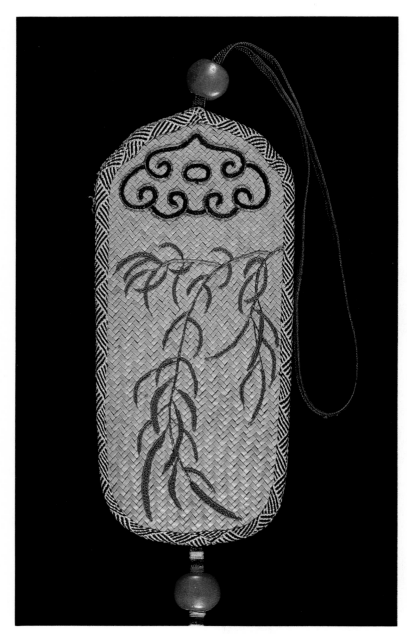

60. Mat-woven spectacles case with willow branches design, embroidered with pulling stitch.

61, 62. Spectacles cases with diamond patterns, embroidered in net stitches.

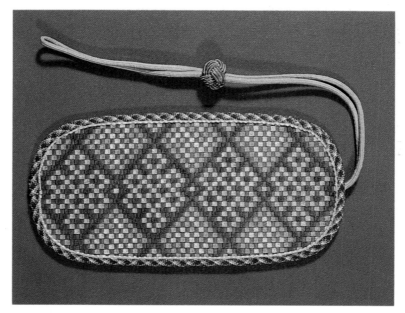

63. Spectacles case with design of a horse, flowers, and rocks, embroidered in various flat stitches.

64. Spectacles case with design of ancient objects, gauze-embroidering.

65. Spectacles case with the character *le* (joy), embroidered by the carving method.

66. Thumb-ring case with the character *le* (joy), embroidered by the carving method.

67. Key case with "infinite happiness" design, couching with palm fibers.

68. Thumb-ring case decorated by couching with gold and silver thread.

Designs on
Clothes

69. Baby's cap decorated with gold-shadowing embroidery.

70. Detail of a baby's cap decorated with gold-shadowing embroidery.

71. Baby's cap with "phoenix amid flowers" design, embroidered in short-straight stitch, consecutive stitch, and carving.

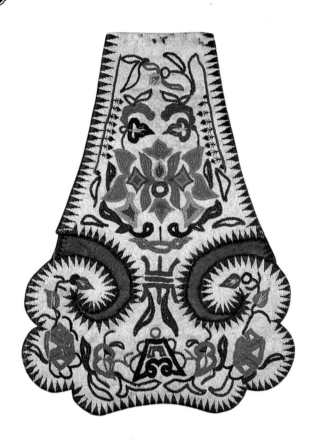

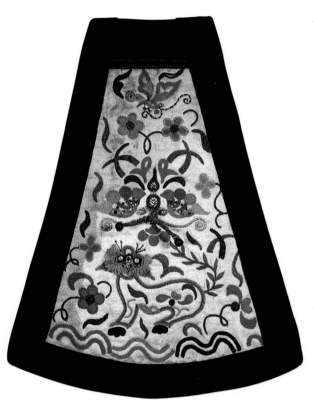

72. Hanging back part of a baby's cap with ornamental curve at each side.

73. Hanging back part of a baby's cap with cat and butterflies, embroidered in pulling stitch, consecutive stitch, winding stitch, couching and piling method.

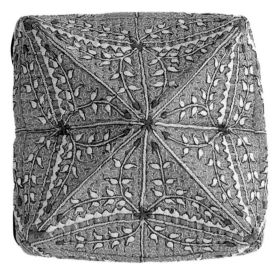

74-76. Embroidered caps of the
Uigur people.

63

77. Collars embroidered in a
    variety of stitches.

78, 79. Gold-decorated collar with ornamental scrolls and a panel picture representing domestic bliss (detail below), embroidered in a large variety of stitches.

80. Collar with four *ruyi* shapes and designs of insects and flowers, embroidered in pulling stitch, consecutive stitch, and many others.

81. Collar with eight *ruyi* shapes, using gauze embroidering, *quanjin* (circling with gold), and knot stitch.

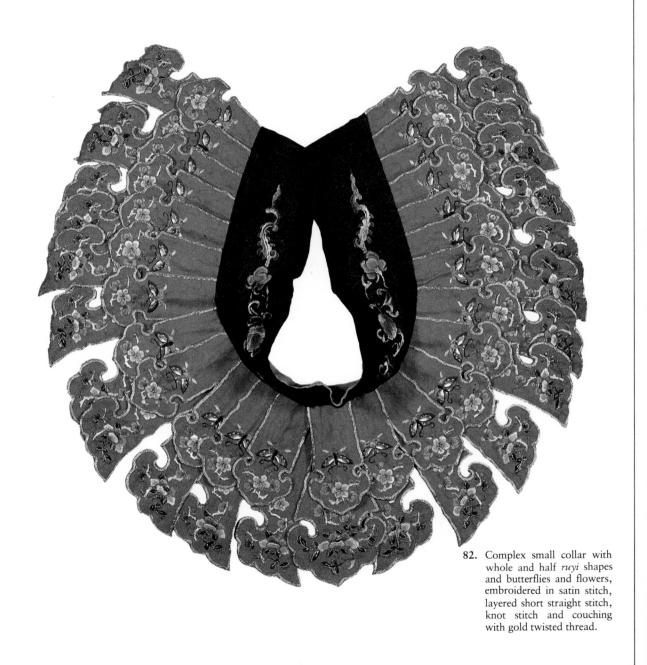

82. Complex small collar with
whole and half *ruyi* shapes
and butterflies and flowers,
embroidered in satin stitch,
layered short straight stitch,
knot stitch and couching
with gold twisted thread.

83. *Ruyi*-shape collar with "two phoenixes worshiping the sun" and "butterflies amid flowers" designs, embroidered in pulling stitch.

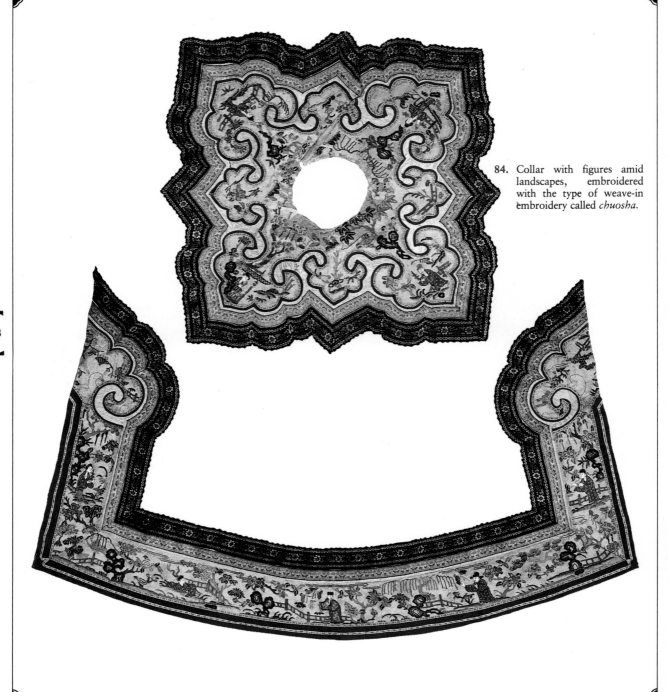

84. Collar with figures amid landscapes, embroidered with the type of weave-in embroidery called *chuosha*.

85, 86. Border of an upper garment (and detail) with
figures amid landscapes,
embroidered with the
type of weave-in em-
broidery called *chuosha*.

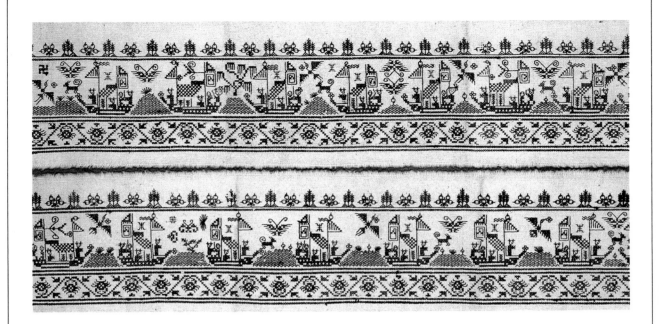

87, 88. Cuff (and detail) with pattern depicting a dragon-boat race, cross-stitch embroidery.

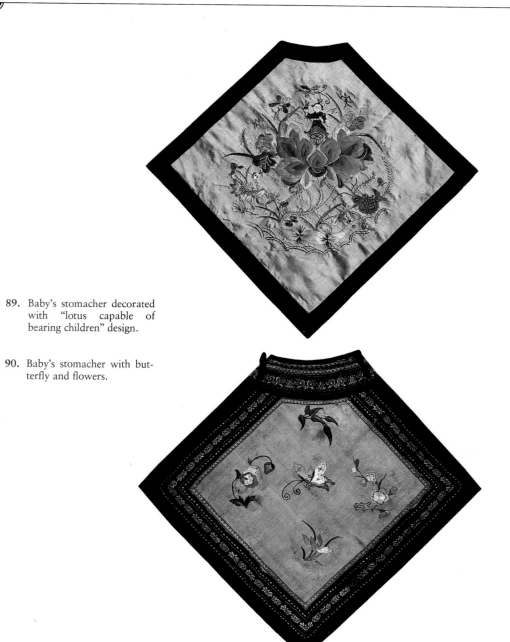

89. Baby's stomacher decorated with "lotus capable of bearing children" design.

90. Baby's stomacher with butterfly and flowers.

91. Embroidered abdomen wrap.

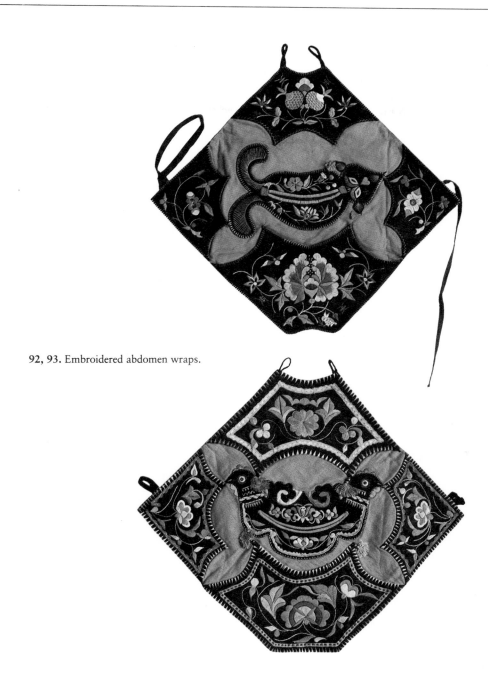

92, 93. Embroidered abdomen wraps.

94, 95. Appliqué designs for skirts.

96, 97. Appliqué designs for skirts.

98, 99. Shawl (and detail) made
by the Hani people in
Yunnan Province.

100, 101. Shoulder bag (and detail) made by the Hani people in Yunnan Province.

102, 103. Shoulder bag (and detail) made by the Hani people in Yunnan Province.

104. Shoes made by the Mongolian people in Yunnan Province.

105. Whimsical shoes in the shape of animals.

106. Shoe uppers with designs depicting local life and scenes from folktales, embroidered in a variety of mainly flat stitches.

107. Shoes, embroidered in satin stitch, *quanjin* method, couching, and knot stitch.

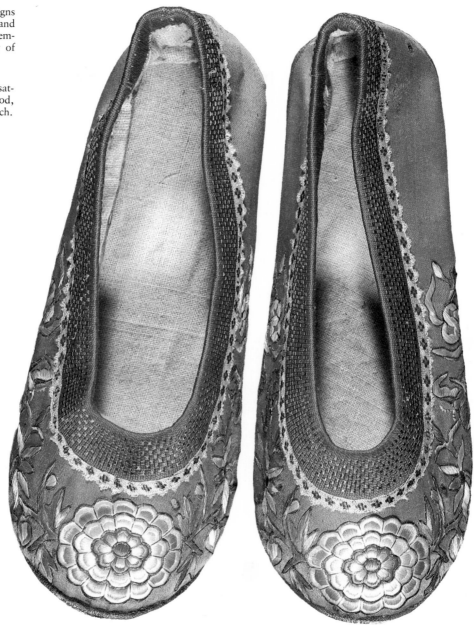

108. Women's puttees, embroidered in satin stitch and couching.

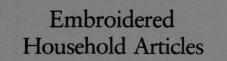

Embroidered
Household Articles

109-112. Door curtain (and details) made in Chaoyang, Liaoning Province.

113. Door curtain made by the Miao people in Hunan Province, cross-stitch embroidery.

114-117. Pillowcases.

118. Pillowcase with rat design, made in Guangyuan, Sichuan Province.

119. Pillow case with crane design, made in Guang-yuan, Sichuan Province.

120. Pillowcase with stylized animal and pine, embroidered mainly in pine-needle and scattering stitches.

121, 122. Pillowcases.

123, 124. Top and side views of a hexagonal box for needles and thread, made in Chaoyang, Liaoning Province.

125. Scissors case.

126. Scissors case, gauze-embroidering.

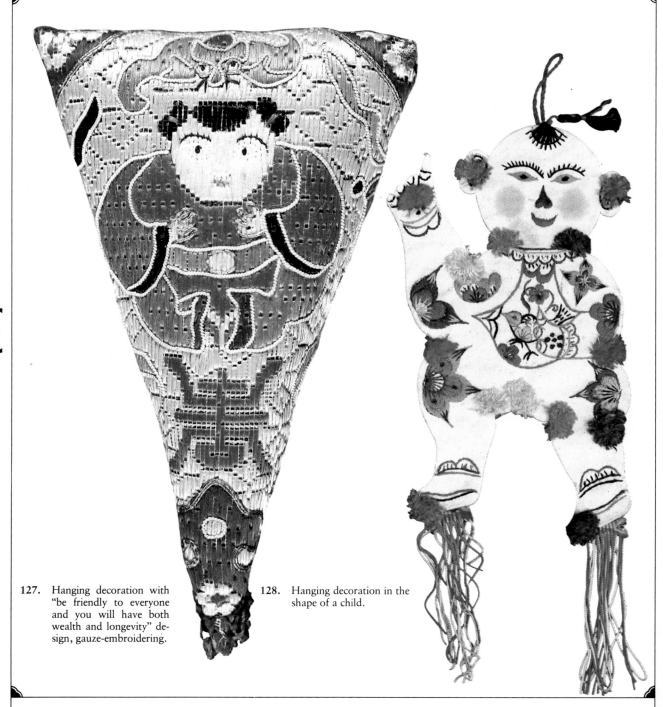

127. Hanging decoration with "be friendly to everyone and you will have both wealth and longevity" design, gauze-embroidering.

128. Hanging decoration in the shape of a child.

129. Hanging decoration in the
       shape of a fan, gauze-
       embroidering.

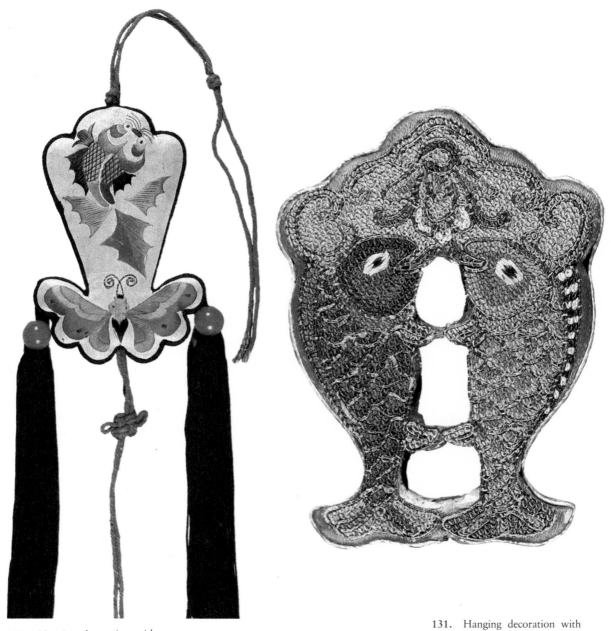

130. Hanging decoration with fish and moth design.

131. Hanging decoration with paired fish design, embroidered in knot stitch.

132, 133. Hanging decorations embroidered over appliquéd padding (the *baohua* technique).

134. Gold-edged hanging decoration with two decorative curves in the middle and designs embroidered in knot stitch.

135. Hanging decoration embroidered over appliquéd padding (*baohua*) and adorned with pearls.

Chinese Embroidery
Designs

136-142 Dragon designs.

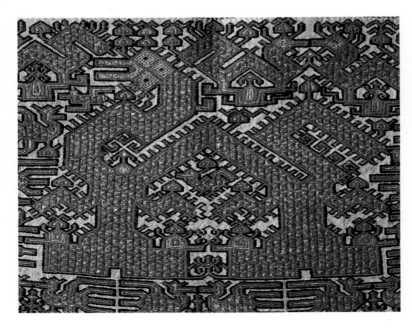

143-149 Phoenix designs

150-155   Flower designs

170-182   Insect designs

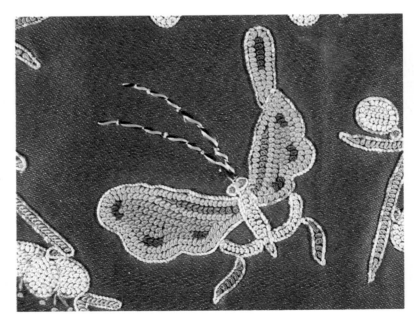

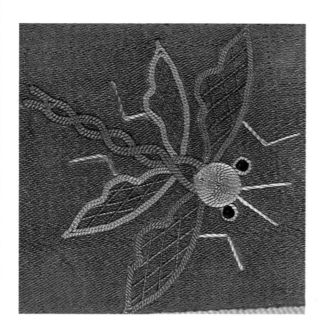

183-189 Fish designs

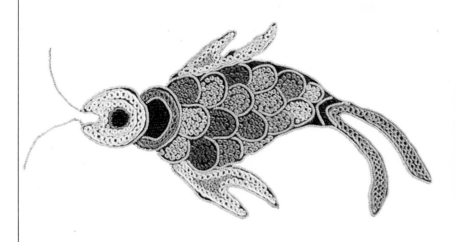

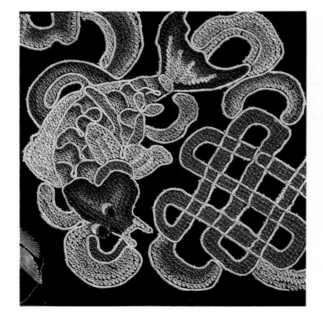

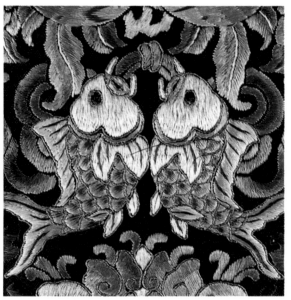

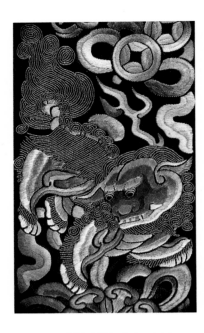

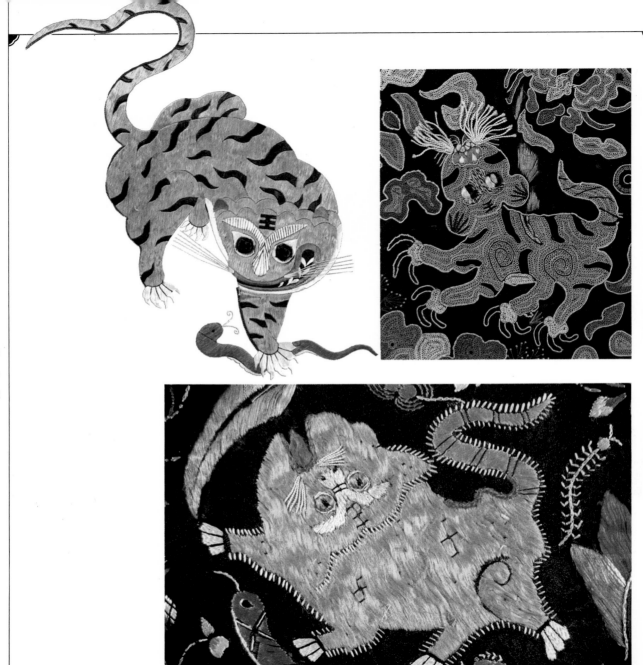

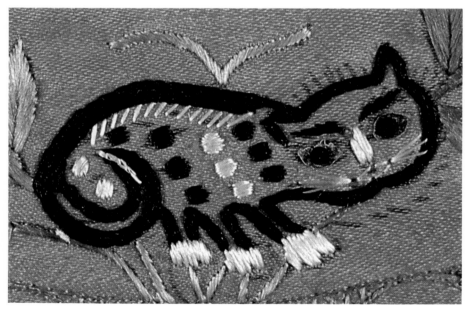

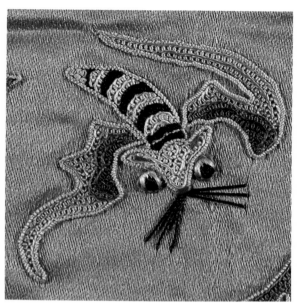

210-222 Human figure designs

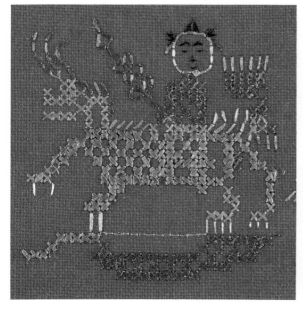

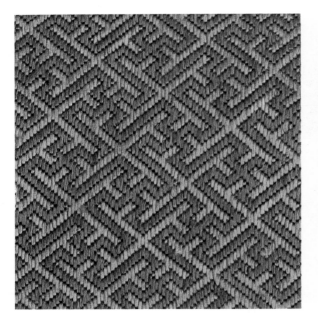

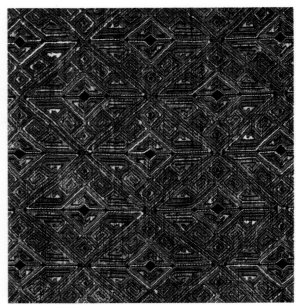

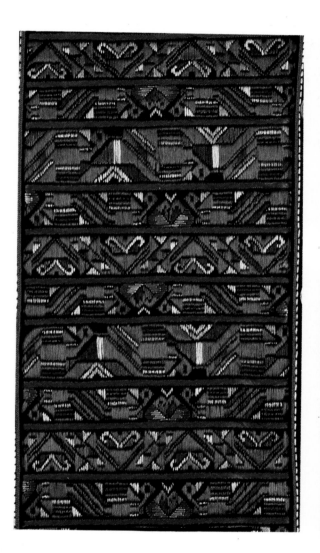

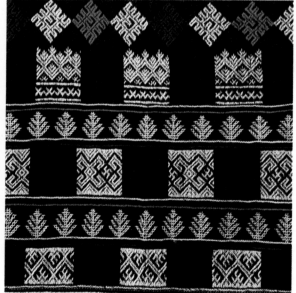

EMBROIDERY
STITCHES

The Embroiderer's Kit

1. Silk thread

2. Tailor's chalk-line bag

3. Pin cushion

4. Embroidery frame

5. Cloth

6. Scissors

7. Unfinished embroidery work

8. Embroidery needles

Primary Stitches and Techniques

Flat Stitchwork

The **satin stitch** (*Fig. 1;* Pls. 33, 45, 63) also known as the even stitch or beyond-the-edge stitch, is a fundamental technique in which the needle rises from one side of the design and falls on the other, filling in the space with short, neat, close, stitches that do not overlap. Tiny flowers or leaves are often embroidered in satin stitch, but large designs can employ this technique as well, by incorporating a ground layer of satin stitches upon which other types of stitches are then overlaid. This makes the design look attractively thick and allows long stitches to be firmly secured. There are several varieties of satin stitch, descriptions of which follow.

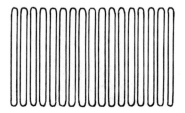

Fig. 1. Satin stitch

The *vertical satin stitch* (*Fig.* 2; Pl. 33) runs vertically across the design.

Fig. 2. Vertical satin stitch

The *horizontal satin stitch* (*Fig.* 3) runs horizontally across the design.

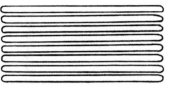

Fig. 3. Horizontal satin stitch

The *slanting satin stitch* (*Fig.* 4; Pl. 47) slants diagonally from left to right, generally at an angle of 45 degrees.

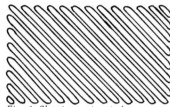

Fig. 4. Slanting satin stitch

The *open fishbone stitch* (*Fig.* 5) goes from left to right, first slanting up and then down to form an inverted V. It is often used to embroider branches, tree leaves, and bird feathers.

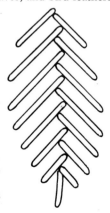

Fig. 5. Open fishbone stitch

The **close-knit stitch** is another common flat-stitching technique, used to create shading or gradations of color. The earliest embroideries exhibiting this skill were found in a Han tomb at Mawangdui, Changsha; the technique became extremely popular in the Tang and Song dynasties. The close-knit stitch is featured in designs blazing with color and is primarily used to make embroidered pictures and reversible Suzhou embroideries. The stitches are arranged so that threads of different color values harmonize or appear to melt into one another, as in *jiese* (joining one color to another) and *xiangse* (adding a color to another to match or enhance the color). Several varieties of close-knit stitch follow.

The *single close-knit stitch* (Fig. 6; Pls. 7, 47) is commonly known as the long-and-short stitch and is generally used to embroider flowers. The stitches are somewhat longer and the threads heavier than those used in many of the other varieties of close-knit stitch.

Fig. 6. Single close-knit stitch

The *double close-knit stitch* (Fig. 7) is used to embroider forms of many different objects. It is longer than the single close-knit stitch except where a line is turned to facilitate the blending of colors, in which case the stitches become shorter. Double close-knit stitch-

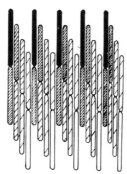

Fig. 7. Double close-knit stitch

es overlap each other, and row after row are tightly knit together to form the design.

The *multiple close-knit stitch* is used to embroider circular designs and tiny round flowers. Stitches of equal length are arranged so that they radiate from a center. The outermost row is stitched first, and successive rows, each closer to the center, are then the circle's center.

The **layered short-straight stitch** or *qiang* stitch, is worked in rows of closely knit, short, straight stitches. Designs can be formed either by stitching the outermost row first and working inward or vice versa. These variations are called the *inward layered short-straight stitch* (Fig. 8) and the *inverse layered short-straight stitch*, respectively. With the inverse method, the border of each row is evenly and tidily trimmed with thread, the color of which conforms to the requirement of the design, changing from darker to lighter to achieve a shaded effect. When designs intersect or overlap, the embroiderer usually leaves a narrow strip of unworked space in between, a technique called voiding. Embroideries made using layered short-straight stitches are durable as well as highly decorative.

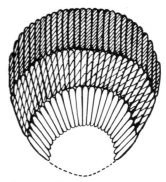

Fig. 8. Inward layered short-straight stitch

The **mixed straight stitch** (Fig. 9), or *chan* stitch, is used to blend and harmonize different colors so that various tones shade into one. Alternate long and short straight stitches radiate from the center of the design, with the working stitches beginning at the middle of the previously worked stitches and spreading out, so there is no hard edge between rows. The colors in a design can gradate from light to dark or vice versa. Because the patterns produced look natural and realistic, this method is often employed to embroider the petals and pistils of large flowers.

Fig. 9. Mixed straight stitch

In the **winding stitch** (Pls. 36, 44), short, slanting stitches pass through the cloth from the back, run across the area, and return to the back of the work in a winding manner. The designs thus produced have clear-cut edges and neat, closely knit stitches. Both the front and back of the embroidery look the same, so there is no "wrong" side. While this is a popular technique, it is not suitable for polychromatic work; embroidery is done using either thread of one color or the graduated tones of one color. The winding stitch is therefore often used to outline regular-shaped, vigorous petals and leaves and to form vibrant lines such as long chrysanthemum petals or the strokes of Chinese characters.

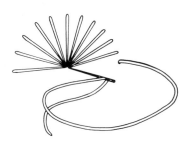

Fig. 10. Pine-needle stitch

The **pine-needle stitch** (*Fig. 10*; Pl. 120) radiates like the ribs of a fan or the spokes of a wheel. All the stitches start from the circumference of the circle and end at the center. In the north of China, this technique is popularly called *basongmi* (forming the pine needles) or *bachegulu* (forming the wheel).

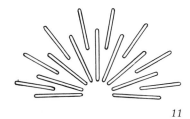

11

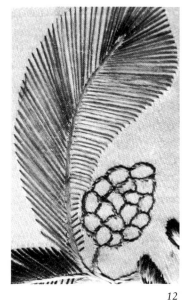

12

Figs. 11, 12. Scattering stitch

The **scattering stitch** (Pl. 120) is worked in either a spread-out fashion (*Fig. 11*) or in a more concentrated form (*Fig. 12*), where the stitches appear like the vane of a feather with its hairs slightly spreading on the outer skirt. (In some places the scattering stitch is called the spreading-out stitch.) It is generally employed to embroider feathers or the leaves of trees.

Fig. 13. Vortex-like pattern stitch

In the **vortex-like pattern stitch** (*Fig. 13*), called *shunxian* (smoothly arranging the threads), the lines are stitched in a twisting or radiating manner. Pleasing effects can be achieved through the proper arrangement of threads; the stitches can be either long or short, called long extending stitches and short extending stitches, respectively.

Embroidering Lines

The **stem stitch** (*Fig. 14*; Pl. 47), also called the rolling stitch, looks like a mid-weight twisted string when finished and is often used to embroider tree branches, ribs of leaves, edges of patterns, and other forceful lines. The stitch is formed in such a way that the starting point for the working stitch is a third of its length away from the back of the previous stitch. Since the stitches twine around each other, the holes made by the needle are concealed.

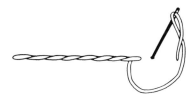

Fig. 14. Stem stitch

The **laced back stitch** (*Fig. 15*), or *biao* (binding) stitch, is made by first embroidering with back stitch, then lacing with a different colored thread and drawing it taut. The result is similar to the stem stitch, but is more durable; when two threads of contrasting colors are used, the resulting lines are quite striking. In northeast China, this technique is usually used to embroider pillow cases and door curtains. I would put this stitch after the back stitch, which is on the next page, because the laced back stitch uses the back stitch as its basis. But this would also require renumbering the drawings.

Fig. 15. Laced back stitch

In the **back stitch** (*Fig. 16*), or *ji* stitch, each working stitch meets the starting point of the previous stitch — the line thus formed is as neat as if it had been drawn with a marker. The back stitch can be made very thin to describe the curved or long, fine lines of fish fins, hair, landscapes, and vines. It is also used for depicting transparent gauze and thin mist. But because the stitch holes are visible, this technique is usually used only to supplement other methods.

Fig. 16. Back stitch

The **running stitch** (*Fig. 17*), or *gong* (pushing) stitch, is a fundamental embroidery skill used to fill in empty spaces. It simply entails pushing the needle through the cloth to create stitches evenly spaced at regular intervals.

Fig. 17. Running stitch

Couching

Couching (*Figs. 18, 19*; Pls. 22, 48, 108) consists of overlaying a heavy single or double thread in a pattern and then fastening it with fine stitches. The fastening thread is thinner than the overlaid thread, and its colors can be used to lend variety to the hue of the design. To distribute the colors evenly, the fastening stitches must be equally spaced and uniform in length.

Couching can be done with a variety of different threads, including gold and silver thread. When single or double gold or silver thread is used to form only the edge of a design, the technique is called **circling with gold** (*quanjin*; Pls. 36, 108) — trim helps to make the design stand out and sometimes to harmonize with the adjacent contrasting colors. When a design is completely overlaid with gold thread, it is called **filling with gold** (*pingjin* or *panjin*; Pls. 30, 58, 59). To soften its harshness and to allow it to reflect different colors, metallic thread can be fastened with a variety of colored threads. Silk thread, palm fiber (*Fig. 20*; Pls. 22, 41, 56, 57, 67), and horsetail thread can all be used for couching.

Fig. 18. Couching

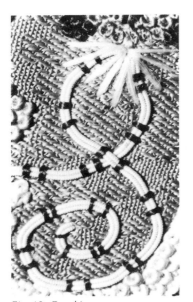

Fig. 19. Couching

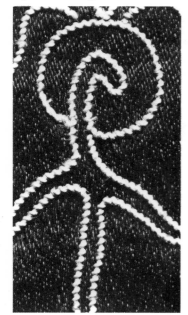

Fig. 20. Couching with palm fibres

The **fastening stitch** is an extensively used method in which long satin stitches are fastened down with one or more straight or slanting short stitches. The purpose is to anchor the long stitches as well as to enhance the beauty of the embroidery.

21

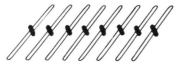

22

Figs. 21, 22. Fastening stitch

Pattern Shaping

The **fur-simulation stitch** is widely used to depict the fur of beasts or the feathers of birds. While strikingly decorative, it is also easy to do. First the ground is covered with flat stitch work (heavier threads are used if the designs are to be in relief). Then thin thread is used to embroider hairlike, straight stitches in short lengths to represent the fur or feathers of animals or birds worked in scattering stitch. The stitches can be either dense or spread out. There is no need to fill in the ground as long as the desired quality is achieved. The short stitches help secure the long groundwork stitches.

Used to embroider eyebrows and eyelashes, the **eyebrow and eyelash stitch** (*Figs. 23, 24*; Pls. 20, 42, 46) is called *bayanjiemao* (making eyelashes). Since it is simple to work, this stitch is extensively used in folk embroidery.

23

24

Figs. 23, 24. Eyebrow and eyelash stitch examples

The **binding stitch** or *le* (curbing) stitch, is used to embroider bird claws. First the ground is covered in straight satin stitches. These are then bound by horizontal stitches, which form the shape of the claw.

There are three types of scale-carving methods, all used to depict the scales of a fish. In the **scale-piling method** (*Fig. 25*), both long and short close-knit stitches are used to form scales that are dark and dense inside with a lighter, thinner edge.

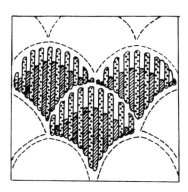

Fig. 25. Scale-piling method

In the **scale-laying**, or *qianglin* (scale-forming) method (*Fig. 26*), the scales are directly embroidered on the cloth in layered short-straight stitches. No groundwork is needed, but one must leave voids (unworked spaces) between the scales.

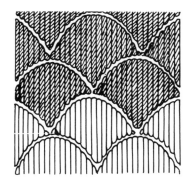

Fig. 26. Scale-laying method

In the **scale-binding method** (*Fig. 27*), a groundwork of vertical satin stitches is divided into scales with back stitches.

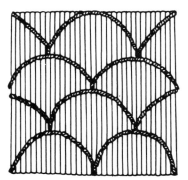

Fig. 27. Scale-binding method

Darning Embroidery

Darning embroidery (*Fig. 28*; Pl. 36), also called *purong* (covering an area with stitches), resembles the hand-weaving of weft-knit brocade. Warp threads of twisted yarn or silk floss are first laid on the ground material, then split silk floss is used as the weft to form geometric designs extending symmetrically from the middle outward; large flowers, too, can be formed in this way. The embroidery is usually worked in bright colors, and the technique to change colors resembles that used in making *zhuanghua* (brocade with flower patterns).

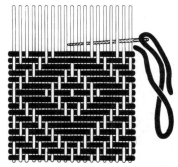

Fig. 28. Darning embroidery

Lay-in brocading (*Figs. 29, 30*), also called *jiajin* or *puyu* (fish-spreading stitch), features a ground fully covered with primarily geometric designs. The designs are first drawn in the shape of squares, triangles, or rhombuses, then embroidering is begun simultaneously from both sides. The colored threads overlap and cross each other until the space is filled in.

29

30

Figs. 29, 30. Lay-in brocading
examples

Weave-in Embroidering

In **gauze-embroidering** (*Figs. 31, 32*;
Pls. 29, 55, 64), called *nasha* or
chuanhua (weaving-in of patterns),
designs are made by passing colored
threads through the mesh of a plain-
colored ground fabric. The ground is
either entirely covered or covered only
in part, in which case the technique is
called *chuosha* (jabbing the fabric; Pls.
84-86). Some say these two methods
are actually one and the same, but
called different names by northerners
and southerners. Gauze-embroidering
was first practiced in the Song dynasty
and it produced some fine work in
both Yuan and Ming days. Under the
reign of Jiaqing in the Qing dynasty, it
became extremely popular.

Embroidery begins with drawing
the designs on the back of the ground
fabric. The designs are then stitched so
they show on the right side, using split
floss thread the thickness of which
conforms to the size of the ground's
mesh. The threads can pass through
the mesh in any manner — vertically,
horizontally, or diagonally. To avoid

Fig. 31. Gauze-embroidery

either damaging the mesh or surface
wrinkling and to achieve the most
pleasing decorative effect, the thread
must be drawn neither too tightly nor
too loosely.

Fig. 32. Gauze-embroidery

The **na stitch** (sewing very close stitches) is worked on a ground already
covered with stitches. The designs,
which consist of patches of color, are
made with double thread and cover the
whole ground. The embroideries
achieved using this technique are extremely durable and can be washed
without the thread breaking or fray-
ing. Pillow slips, curtains, tablecloths,
and door curtains are all embroidered
by this method.

Pulling Embroidery

In the **pulling stitch** (*Figs. 33, 34*; Pls. 38, 184), or silk-locking stitch, two threads are used simultaneously. The first thread coils on the surface of the ground cloth to form patterns; the second thread, usually thinner than the first, secures the loops. Embroidery begins by passing both threads through the cloth from the back at a small distance from each other. The first thread is wound around the second needle in a counterclockwise direction to form a loop, which is then anchored with a back stitch made with the second thread. After this, the second thread is once more passed through the cloth, and another counterclockwise loop made with the first thread; this loop is back-stitched with the second thread as before. The process is repeated until the desired effect is achieved. Changing the thickness and colors of the threads may produce pleasing results, and since the stitch is durable as well as beautiful, it is widely employed in making folk embroideries for everyday use.

If the two threads crisscross right and left to form two strings of loops (*Figs. 35, 36*) secured to the ground material, the result is a **double pulling stitch** (Pls. 27, 28).

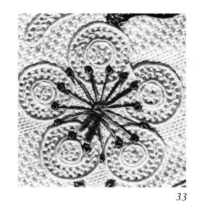

33

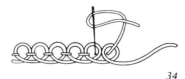

34

Figs. 33, 34. Pulling stitch

35

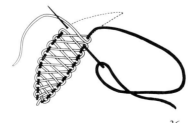

36

Figs. 35, 36. Double pulling stitch

The **coiling stitch** (*Figs. 37, 38*; Pls. 27, 28) is also made with two threads. The first thread coils around a tiny round stick or a very thick thread (which acts as a knitting needle) to form loops, and is back-stitched in place by the second thread. Thick double thread is used for coiling, while thinner thread is used for back-stitching. After being removed from the stick, the loops are positioned into designs. The thread can be changed whenever necessary to give the desired effect. Because this technique is time-consuming, it is seldom used, but it is extremely decorative and unmatched in beauty when used to embroider flowers in relief.

37

38

Figs. 37, 38. Coiling stitch

Chain Embroidery

The **chain stitch** (*Fig. 39*; Pls. 2, 6, 217), also called the linking stitch or *suohua* (locking of patterns), is formed by linking rings of silk together in chains. Patterns formed by this method are durable and highly decorative, with resilient lines and clear-cut edges in relief. Chain-stitching is simple to do and one of the oldest techniques in Chinese embroidery. The earliest example dates back to the Western Zhou dynasty (Pl. 1); later embroideries discovered in a Western Han tomb at Dabaotai, Beijing, also show chain stitches (*Fig. 40*).

Because of its relatively open weave, a chain-stitched surface is necessarily matte, but it is definitely not lackluster. Rather, embroidery done in chain stitch has a calm, dignified appearance that does much to enhance the overall beauty of the design. As the effect of satin stitchwork made with split floss can be likened to flashing satin, embroideries done in chain stitch can be compared to silk gauze. Though colors contrast more sharply in chain stitch than in satin stitch, with artful blending this is by no means unpleasant to the eye.

There are a number of variations of the chain stitch.

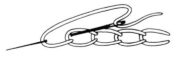

Fig. 39. *Chain stitch*

Fig. 40. *Part of a chain-stitched embroidery found in a Western Han tomb at Dabaotai, Beijing*

In the *close-ring chain stitch* (*Fig. 41*), the needle rises from and falls into the same needle hole to form small chains of rings. The *open-ring chain stitch* (*Fig. 42*) forms chains with large rings. *The double-ring chain stitch* (*Fig. 43*) is used to form a chain with strongly locked edges, in which the rings are fastened closely together.

Fig. 41. *Close-ring chain stitch*

Fig. 42. *Open-ring chain stitch*

Fig. 43. *Double-ring chain stitch*

Unlinked, separate rings are made by the **daisy stitch,** also called the detached chain stitch or single-ring stitch (*Figs. 44, 45*). When the stitches take the form of a curve crossing itself, they are called **loop stitches** (*Fig. 46*). The **half ring stitch** (*Figs. 47-49*), or the fly stitch, or the feather stitch are made like the chain stitch, but the ends of each ring are far apart. These stitches can be worked separately or joined together to form designs, which are often used for edging.

Fig. 44. *Daisy stitch*

Fig. 45. *Daisy stitch*

Fig. 46. *Loop stitch*

47

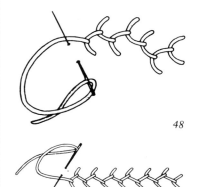

48

49

Figs. 47-49 Half-ring stitch examples

In the **braid stitch** (*Fig. 50*), otherwise known as strands of braids, the needle passes through the thread itself to form the first ring (instead of passing through the ring as in the double-ring chain stitch), and connects the first ring with the second. This goes on until the rings are locked together like hair braids. This form of chain stitch is usually made with heavy thread and is used for edging; where this is the case, the braid is sometimes reinforced with another chain. When edging a long border, the embroiderer will usually change the color of the thread section by section in accordance with the design. Symmetrical designs usually have edges on both sides. This method is widely used among the Miao people in Guizhou.

Fig. 50. Braid stitch

The **blanket stitch** (*Fig. 51*), called the edge-sealing stitch or button-locking, is often used to embroider buttonholes and the edges of clothing in small and medium designs. It is also used in the methods of *baohua* (padded embroidery) and carving. When used to secure gold thread, this technique is called *suojin* (locking of gold).

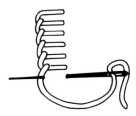

Fig. 51. Blanket stitch

The **consecutive stitch** (*Fig. 52*), called the split stitch, is in fact a simplified chain stitch, so it is also popularly known as the fake stitch. Instead of being formed by rings, the chain is created by passing a back stitch through the end of the previous stitch and splitting it in two. The consecutive stitch can be used on its own, but in ancient times it was often used together with the chain stitch to embroider thin lines.

Fig. 52. Consecutive stitch

Knotting

The **knot stitch** (*Figs. 53-56*; Pls. 20, 32, 40, 44), also known as ring embroidering, is a simple method to form shiny designs in relief. More than twenty varieties of knot stitch can be found throughout history — the knots can be large or tiny and, among other patterns, are extremely useful for forming the pistils of flowers, animals, and figures. Early relics of this stitch have been found in an Eastern Han tomb unearthed at Nuoyinwula, Outer Mongolia, but even earlier examples are the decorative knots on a pair of silk shoes discovered in a tomb of the Warring States period in Linzi, Shandong Province. Knot-stitching is particularly useful for objects that wear out easily, such as small bags (Pls. 20, 35), *dalian* (a bag sewn at both ends with an opening in the middle; Pls. 36-39), seat cushions, and children's shoes (Pl. 105).

Fig. 53. Knot stitch

54

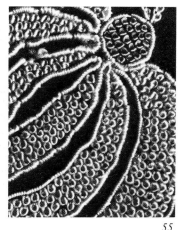

55

Figs. 54, 55. Knot stitch examples

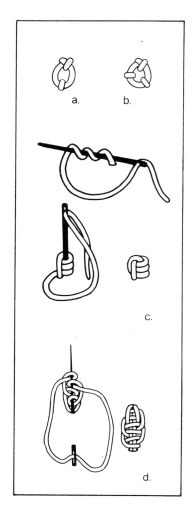

a.   b.

c.

d.

Fig. 56. Four types of knot stitch

Netting

The **net stitch** (*Figs. 57-62*; Pls. 54, 61, 62) is also called *huazhenxiu* or *wenzhenxiu* (both meaning pattern embroidery). Among the Miao people, it is known as *banhua* (pulling designs). Net-stitching may be done on a ground of gauze having a regular mesh; designs are embroidered by passing thread through the mesh. When tightly woven material is used for the ground, straight or slanting threads, or checks, can be sewn upon it, and then further designs embroidered on top of these threads. Designs worked on a meshed ground often give the effect of a hollowed-out carving, but those embroidered on a closely woven fabric appear as if covered with an extremely thin patterned curtain. Designs embroidered in net stitch should be surrounded by a border of stem stitches or by couching of gold or silver thread. In designs formed by the combined use of net stitch and other techniques, the net-stitched parts should likewise be bordered. Whether used alone or with other methods, net-stitching can create beautiful patterns, and objects embroidered using this technique are in great demand.

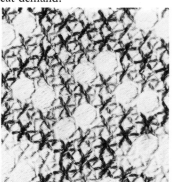

Fig. 57. Net stitch

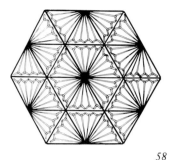

58

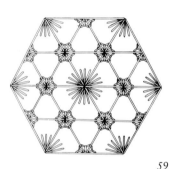

59

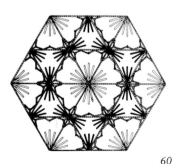

60

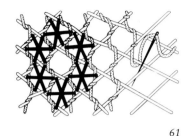

61

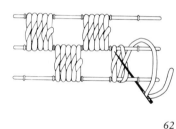

62

Figs. 58-62. Net stitch examples

Cross-Stitching

The **cross stitch** (*Figs. 63-65*; Pls. 87, 88, 113) called *tiaohua* (picking patterns) or *tiaoluo* (stitching in gauze), is an ancient technique of using crosses to form a design. During embroidery, the crosses should be kept the same size and be neatly arranged as well as evenly spaced. Great care must be taken while working, for if too much force is used to pull the thread, the ground material will wrinkle. But if too little force is used, the design will become misshapen and furred, which will affect the embroidery's appearance and durability. The open fishbone stitch is sometimes used as a substitute for the cross stitch, but because of the rigidity of its shape, it is not as popular.

Both monochromatic and polychromatic threads are used in cross-stitching, but monochromatic work is preferred. Cross stitched embroidery is durable, highly decorative, and easy to make, and is widely used by minority peoples in China to decorate the aprons, pillowcases, and handkerchiefs of peasant women.

63

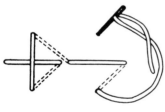

64

65

Figs. 63-65. Cross stitch

Edging

How an embroidery is edged can greatly affect its quality. Edges not only heighten the decorative effect of the designs but also make the embroidery more durable, so they are very important.

The edging skills used in folk embroidery are numerous. The most popular patterns include hound's-tooth, cucumber trellises, and lotus leaves, but a variety of more complicated methods also exists. The drawings illustrate four techniques: front, back (*Fig. 66*); lattice pattern (*Fig. 67*); hound's-tooth pattern (*Fig. 68*); and chevron stitch (*Fig. 69*). *Figures 70* and *71* show additional examples.

Fig. 66. Edging examples

Fig. 67. Lattice-pattern edging

Fig. 68. Hound's-tooth edging

Fig. 69. Chevron stitch edging

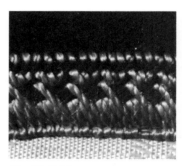

Fig. 70. Edging

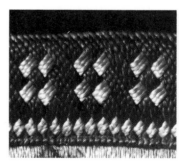

Fig. 71. A complicated variety of edging called koubian

144

Other Techniques

Appliqué (Pls. 94-97), known as *buhua* (patch pattern) or *tieling* (adding damask silk), is the process of adding cutout designs of exotic material to a ground material. When cutout patterns are used to pad embroidery designs, the method is called *baohua* (Pls. 132, 133) — before embroidering, the cotton or silk pads are fastened along their edges to the ground material using blanket stitches or other straight stitches. Though very simple, appliqué can produce attractive results and is therefore widely used either on its own or with other methods.

The **piling method** (*Fig.* 72; Pl 38) is also called high-rising embroidery or padding, because a part of the design is raised higher than the rest. This is done by adding layers of heavy thread, cotton, or a pad of paper fastened with single close-knit stitches. The raised part is then covered with stitches to produce realistic designs in relief.

In the **carving method** (*Figs.* 73, 74; Pls. 65, 66), called *diaoxiu*, long stitches are first sewn around the edges of the design with heavy thread; this thread is then covered with blanket or winding stitches so that the designs will be raised above the ground material. The parts to be hollowed are then cut out with a small pair of scissors. To add to the complexity of the design, a piece of thin gauze can be placed over the carved areas or additional designs can be net-stitched in those areas. The objects produced by this method can either be completely carved (with the entire design hollowed out) or partially carved. *Figure 74* shows a completely carved spectacle case. The case was first embroidered with knot stitches and couching of palm fibers, then it was cut out according to the design. Objects usually look more beautiful, subtle, and elegant when the same color is used both for the thread and the ground material.

Fig. 74. Carving method

The **random stitch** consists of embroidering with irregularly arranged straight stitches to depict a part of a design. It might have been invented to imitate the shading of embroidered paintings. The trees in *Riding a Crane over a Beautiful Terrace* (Pl. 12), a Southern Song embroidered painting preserved by the Museum of Liaoning Province, are a good example of this technique.

Double-face embroidery (two-face embroidery) looks the same on both sides. It is usually done with close-knit stitches; the places where the thread passes in and out of the ground material should be well concealed so as not to spoil the effect. The embroideries done by the Miao people in Guizhou and Sichuan provinces have identical regular geometric patterns on both sides of the cloth. They call the method *limianhua* (inside-pattern making) or *xianhua* (small-pattern making) and use monochromatic single threads either as the weft or warp to form elegant designs.

Fig. 72. Piling method

Fig. 73. Carving method

Shadow embroidery, or *tuodixiu* (groundless embroidery), is worked on a piece of thin, transparent material: stitches made on the back of the ground fabric produce a shadowy design on the front. This kind of embroidery is unique and delicately charming.

Ground-borrowing embroidery, also known as *jiedixiu,* means "supplementing the effect of the design by ground color." During embroidery, blanks are purposely left on the ground material as part of the design.

Color-borrowing embroidery is also called *jiesexiu* or half-embroidery-half-painting because parts of the design are painted on with brushes. This method saves time and labor, especially when only the major designs are embroidered and the rest is left to the painter. Sometimes only the outline of a pattern is embroidered, and sometimes colors are added to achieve the right tone for the picture — many different methods are involved.

In **gold-shadowing embroidery** (Pl. 69), or *yingjin*, stitches are worked on a design already covered with gold foil so that golden light will glisten forth from between them. This method creates an opulent look and is widely used in Guangdong embroidery.

In **core-wrapping embroidery**, or *baogeng (Fig. 75)*, a heavy core line is wound with silk thread or blanket-stitched *(Fig. 76)*, or worked in eyelet holes *(Fig. 77)*, depending on the design. The core line can be made with running stitches using thick core thread or other materials. Care should be taken not to draw the thread too tightly or too loosely. The em-

broidered lines rise in relief; when the design is hollowed, the embroidery will become carved.

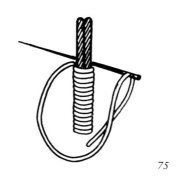

75

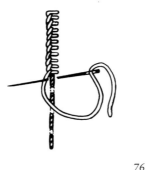

76

77

Figs. 75-77. Core-wrapping embroidering

Woolen yarn embroidery consists of using woolen yarn instead of silk floss and coarse linen for the ground. The designs are made by gauze-embroidering, passing the yarn through the mesh of the ground material. Embroideries thus made are durable and greatly favored.

Wool-cutting embroidery, or *jianrongxiu,* requires a special needle (a large syringe needle can be adapted). Needle and yarn pass through the ground material from the back to make close-knit stitches along the edge of the design, forming numerous loops. These loops are then cut to give the embroidery a downy appearance. This technique is usually employed to embroider the uppers of children's shoes and pillow slips and is used everywhere in the North China countryside.

Drawn work is created by removing particular warp or weft threads from the ground fabric and then tying the remaining threads with various stitches to form open designs resembling lace. Drawn work has become an independent embroidery form, with its own exclusive set of skills. The grounds typically used are plain-woven linen and cotton cloth, and objects worked with this method include tablecloths, chair covers, handkerchiefs, and clothing.

In **pearl embroidering** *(Fig. 78;* Pl. 135), otherwise known as pearl threading or pearl fastening, tiny pearls or glass beads are strung together, coiled along the edges of the design, and immediately couched on the ground cloth to form patterns. The thread used for couching must be extremely strong to withstand tension during stitching. Where the string is positioned in a straight line, it is fastened at intervals of eight or ten pearls, but where the string twists and turns, stitches are made behind every first or second pearl. Embroideries made in this way have brilliant luster and are usually used for theatrical costumes, ladies' clothing, and bags.

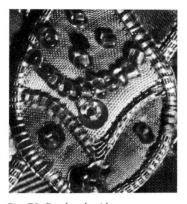

Fig. 78. Pearl embroidery

In **spangle-fastening,** gold foil or shining round or rectangular sequins (*Fig. 79*) are used to brighten the design and add luster to the work. This is a common technique in folk embroidery.

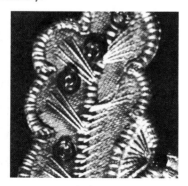

Fig. 79. Spangle-fastening

Decorative Knots

Decorative knots are ornamental plaiting done with silk thread or cord and are attached to objects or worn at the waist as part of such things as small bags and spectacle cases. There are many varieties. The few examples here include the **flat square knot** (*Fig. 80*), the **long knot** (*Fig. 81*), the **abacus bead knot** (*Fig. 82*), and the **butterfly knot** (*Figs. 83, 84*).

Fig. 80. Flat square knot

Fig. 81. Long knot

Fig. 82. Abacus bead knot

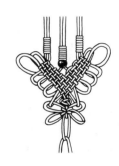

83

84

Figs. 83, 84. Butterfly knots

Table of Primary Stitches and Techniques

Category	Stitch	Other Names	Earliest Specimen
flat stitchwork	satin stitch	even, straight, beyond-the-edge	found in a Western Han tomb at Mawangdui
	vertical satin stitch		
	horizontal satin stitch		
	slanting satin stitch		
	open fishbone stitch		an Eastern Han relic found at Nuoyinwula
	spreading stitch	vertical, horizontal, slanting	
	close-knit stitch	stick-in, long-and-short	found in a Western Han tomb at Mawangdui
	single close-knit stitch		
	double close-knit stitch		
	multiple close-knit stitch		
	layered short-straight stitch	*qiang*	Tang dynasty
	inward layered short-straight stitch	inward *qiang*	
	inverse layered short-straight stitch	inverse *qiang*	
	mixed straight stitch	*chan, can, souhe*	Southern Song embroidery *Riding a Crane over a Beautiful Terrace*
	winding stitch	*rao*	found in a Liao tomb at Yemaotai
	pine-needle stitch	*basongmi* (forming the pine needles),	Southern Song embroidery *Riding a Crane over a Beautiful Terrace*
	wheel stitch	*bachequlu* (forming the wheel)	
	scattering stitch	spreading-out	Southern Song embroidery *Riding a Crane over a Beautiful Terrace*
	vortex-like pattern stitch	*shunxian*	
embroidering lines	stem stitch	rolling, rod-like, biting, *bi*, pulling, willow	Southern Song embroidery *Riding a Crane over a Beautiful Terrace*
	laced back stitch	*biao*	
	back stitch	*ji, qie,* stabbing	embroidered images of Buddha in Mogao Cave made in Northern Wei dynasty

Category	Stitch	Other Names	Earliest Specimen
	running stitch	*gong*	
couching	silk thread	mixed thread	found in a Liao tomb at Yemaotai
	palm fiber		
	horse-tail thread		
	circling with gold or silver (*quanyin* or *quanjin*)		found in a Liao tomb at Yemaotai
	filling with gold or silver (*panjin* or *panyin*)	*pinggin* or *pingyin*	Southern Song embroidery *Riding a Crane over a Beautiful Terrace*
	fastening stitch	fixing	Southern Song embroidery *Riding a Crane over a Beautiful Terrace*
pattern shaping	fur-simulation stitch	simulation, fur making	found in Huang Sheng's tomb (Southern Song) at Fuzhou
	eyebrow and eyelash stitch	*bayanjiemao*	
	binding stitch	*le*	
	scale-piling method		
	scale-laying method	*qianglin*	
	scale-binding method		found in the Yuan city of Jininglu
darning embroidery	darning embroidery (*purong*)	*tiaoxiu, pujin, bierong,* knitting	
	lay-in brocading (*jiajin*)	*puyu*	Southern Song embroidery *Riding a Crane over a Beautiful Terrace*
weave-in embroidering	gauze-embroidering	*nasha, kaidijin, chuanhua*	found in a Song tomb at Shanxi
	chuosha		found in a Song tomb at Shanxi
	na stitch		
pulling embroidery	pulling stitch	lock forming, pulling golden lock, winding-thread, pulling and winding, silk-locking, coiling, connecting	
	double pulling stitch		
	coiling stitch		
chain embroidery	chain stitch	*chuanhua, taohua, suohua, luohua, kouhua, lahua,* close-knit, linking, strands of braids	found in a Western Zhou tomb at Rujiazhuang, Baoji

Category	Stitch	Other Names	Earliest Specimen
	close-ring chain stitch		
	open-ring chain stitch		
	double-ring chain stitch		
	daisy stitch	detached chain single-ring	found in Chu tomb No.1 at Mashan, Jiangling
	loop stitch		found in a Western Han tomb at Dabaotai
	half-ring stitch	fly stitch, feather stitch	found in Chu tomb No.1 at Mashan, Jiangling
	braid stitch	strands of braids	
	blanket stitch	edge-sealing, sealing-the-openings, *wenming* edge, button-locking	
	suojin		
	consecutive stitch	split, fake	an Eastern Han relic found at Luobunaoer
knotting	knot stitch (*dazi*)	making knots, knots, ring embroidering, point	found in a Warring States tomb in Liwzi, Shandong Province.
	double knot stitch	wheat grain	
netting	net stitch	*huazhenxiu, wenzhenxiu, banhua,* knitting	Southern Song embroidery *Riding a Crane over a Beautiful Terrace*
cross-stitching	cross	*tiaohua, jiahua,* strings of crosses, *tiaoluo, laling, piehua*	an Eastern Han relic found at Nuoyinwula
	open fishbone stitch		
edging	hound's-tooth		
	lattice pattern		
	cucumber trellises		
	chevron stitch		
	lotus leaves		
	edge sealing		
	soujin		
	edge adding		

Category	Stitch	Other Names	Earliest Specimen
other techniques	appliqué	*buhua, tiejuan, tieling*	found in Huang Sheng's tomb (Southern Song) at Fuzhou
	baohua	embossed patterns	
	piling method	padding, high-rising	
	carving method (*diaoxiu*)	hollowing-out	
	random stitch		Southern Song embroidery *Riding a Crane over a Beautiful Terrace*
	double-face embroidery	two-face *limianhua, xianhua*	
	shadow embroidery	*tuodixiu*	
	ground-borrowing embroidery (*jiedixiu*)		
	color-borrowing embroidery	*jiesexiu,* half-embroidery-half-painting	Southern Song embroidery *Riding a Crane over a Beautiful Terrace*
	gold-shadowing embroidery	*yingjin*	
	core-wrapping embroidery (*baogeng*)		
	woolen-yarn embroidery		
	wool-cutting embroidery	*jianrongxiu*	
	gerongxiu		
	drawn work		
	pearl embroidering	pearl threading, pearl fastening	
	spangle-fastening		found in a Liao tomb at Yemaotai
decorative knots	flat square knot		
	long knot		
	abacus bead		
	butterfly knot		

APPENDICES

Embroidery in the Chaoyang District, Liaoning Province

by Wang Yarong

233. Li Dianzhi twisting a horse-tail thread.

In November 1982 I took part in the excavation of Jin tombs, undertaken by the Liaoning Provincial Museum. This afforded me the opportunity to meet several folk embroidery artists, all women, living in Chaoyang County: Li Dianzhi, Mrs. Wei, and Zhou Zixian.

Fifty-eight-year-old Li Dianzhi was my landlady and a very warm-hearted woman. My interest in embroidery pleased her so much that she took the trouble to rummage through her chests and cupboards and found some old embroidered works of hers, such as a butterfly pincushion (see page 130), purse with the design of old coins (Illustration No. 21), a key-bag, and many others. She recalled in detail her keen interest in embroidery when she was a young girl and the kinds of embroidery objects she had made. She even taught me some of the various techniques she used, such as twisting the "the horse-tail thread." As if by heredity, her daughter, Fengling, also loved embroidery. Embroidery objects of everyday use decorated with modern patterns filled the room. It is a shame that she used only one technique, *jianrongxiu,* or wool-cutting embroidering (see page 146).

Accompanied by Fengling, I went to a remote mountain gully called Halahai, where her grandmother lived. It was with great difficulty that we finally found Zhou Zixian, a master hand in embroidery well known throughout Chaoyang some decades ago. She was famous for her *purongnajin,* or darning embroidery (see page 137). Seventy-nine years of age, but still clear-minded and witty, she was a woman with an artistic disposition. Sadly this one-time master of embroidery had become totally blind. I owe much to this old woman for what I know about the folk embroidery in Chaoyang. She was very excited about my interest in her past career as an embroiderer and recalled with nostalgia the best embroideries she had made when she had been a girl and a bride and how they were appreciated by other people. She even told me of her method for handling silk thread, which she had formerly kept to herself: when embroidering with split silk threads, first pass the thread through a honey locust previously steeped in water before threading a needle. The thread will then look as if waxed. Embroidery objects using such threads will wear well and look smooth and shiny. If there is no honey locust, onions will also do. Perhaps this was the first time after so many years that she had had a willing listener ready to lend an ear to her talk about embroidery. She was especially pleased with me, even asking permission to run her hand over my face to know exactly what I looked like, so as to remember her "young friend." I was most willing to let her touch my face. Watching the pair of eyes that at one time must have been very bright, I was touched to tears. When I asked her whether she still kept any of her embroidered works, she told me regretfully that the last pair of pillow slips had been given to her second daughter when the latter got married. After a short pause, however, she took her walking stick and said, "Come on. Let's go to my second daughter's." Though the aged woman had not stirred out of doors for many years, and despite the icy wind, she did not hesitate to take me to a small village about ten *li* away, where her second daughter resided. Her daughter, who had been married for thirty years, had never used the treasured pillow slips until recently, when her own son was about to get married. When I saw the fine embroidery pieces that she had done with her own hands (see Pls. 102, 103), I could not help being filled with respect and love for this folk artist whom few people know. I was very lucky that day, for the old woman even succeeded in persuading her daughter to part with this last piece of embroidery when we left. She said that she felt more at ease with the pillow slips in my care, and that she wanted to make friends with me.

The experience remains vivid in my memory even today, as I recall my visit to

Chaoyang, and I am very glad to take this chance to introduce my esteemed old friends and their works to the readers.

The following is a brief survey of the folk embroidery in Chaoyang. Most of the surviving famous embroidered works were done by local master needlewomen before their marriage, and there are ample quantities for reference today. Following the custom prevalent in Hebei and Shandong provinces, a girl in the locality when getting married was required to display a considerable number of embroidered works, which not only proved the bride's skill and cleverness, but became the best presents to her husband's relatives when she met them for the first time. These included door curtains (consisting of two kinds — "double *yaozi*" and "single *yaozi*," *yaozi* being a term for the decoration, in single or double row, embroidered on the top end of the curtain) and *baohua* curtains (curtains with designs couched on them). These large pieces were hung at the door during festivals. They could also be hung on walls on ordinary days. Then there were embroidered window curtains cupboard covers, clock covers, shoes, key cases, pin cushions, scissors cases, pouches for tailor's chalk lines, table cloths, pouches for needles and thread, pillow slips and many other embroideries, which were used to decorate clothes, caps and mirror covers. There were also objects embroidered with the likenesses of characters in Chinese legends or in plays performed in the locality.

The embroidery technique used in Chaoyang consists mainly of satin stitching. But when the stitch is too long, the embroiderer will usually add an additional stitch in the middle or sew *na* stitches, which do not run and wash well.

There are two types of embroidery — monochrome and multicolored. Of the first type there are, for instance, blue curtains, the *yaozi* of which are made of patterns imitating the flowers of four seasons, all stitched in white (peony, water lily, chrysan-

234. Purse with a design of ancient coins, embroidered by Li Dianzhi.

themum, and plum in four bunches). White curtains are used only when a family is in mourning. Multi-colored embroideries are numerous.

Plied silk yarn is the chief type of thread used in embroidering. The local people call it "whole thread," while they call split floss "broken thread," In Chaoyang, silk floss split into four is the thinnest thread used. To twist a "horse-tail thread," a hair is taken from a horse's tail, and its end attached to that of a split thread. The free end of the split thread is then held between the teeth. The end of the horse-tail hair connected to the split thread is held in the right hand and the other end in the left. Next the thread is twisted with the fingers of the right hand, with the left hand acting in unison. In this way, the split thread spirals around the whole length of the horse-tail hair. After that, a hard knot is tied at the end. The horse-tail thread thus made twists like the letter Z. Another kind of horse-tail thread that twists in an S shape is made by pinning one end of the split thread on a quilt. A dark horse tail is suitable for a deep-colored horse-tail thread, and a white horse tail for a light-colored one. Horse-tail thread is usually used to trim the edges of embroidered designs or to harmonize two strongly contrasting colors. The technique employed in trimming is the same as that used in couching.

The main stitch types used in Chaoyang number no less than thirteen. The designs on the embroidery articles are just as varied. Those on door curtains include the following: "Liu Hai scattering coins," "magpies perching on a plum branch," "fish swimming beside a water lily" (symbolizing harmony), "phoenix playing with a peony," and "lions playing with a silk ball." Couching is the usual technique used. Decorative articles like pillow slips are mostly embroidered with characters adorned with floral designs (Pl. 235). Other designs include "a hundred seeds contained in a pomegranate ", * "happiness and longevity" (represented by coins), "phoenix facing the sun," "red plum with seeds," * "bamboo and its shoots," * "pine trees and cranes" (symbols of longevity), "two dragons playing with a pearl," and "unicorn tending its young." Flowers of the four seasons are also common themes. Objects with designs embroidered in relief include ear muffs and pouches for tailor's chalk lines. Their designs are mostly a triangular *ruyi* (an S-shaped symbol of good luck), a butterfly, a pup, a fish or a calabash. Embroideries done with couching techniques supplemented by stitching or painting represent another major type. Characters in Chinese legends symbolizing longevity and good luck are the motifs usually used. The borders of embroideries are mostly decorated with motifs of "water ripple," "cucumber trellis," and others.

Whether in designs, colors or varieties, the embroidery in Chaoyang is a distinctive type of folk embroidering art in North China, possessing many unique features, and is therefore worthy of our research and study.

January, 1985
(Translated by Shi Huiqing)

---

* All symbolize offspring in plenty

235. Pillowcase embroidered with characters adorned with floral designs.

156

The Embroidering Career of My Grandmother

by Wulianghai Suhe

The embroidered images of Buddha shown on the following two pages (Pls. 237-39) were done by my grandmother. Though they cannot show the full range of her skills, they nevertheless show the unique style of Mongolian embroidery.

My grandmother was born in 1860 into a distinguished family in Wengniute District. Her family name was Baoerjigude and her given name Cailajina (Pl. 236). She died in 1949. She was intelligent and dextrous when still a child. As she grew up, she began to learn needlework with her mother. At first she learned sewing but later she concentrated on the study of Mongolian traditional embroidery. The boots, pouches, and small bags she embroidered in her teens were already admired for their ingenious design and fine workmanship. Her marriage with my grandfather was an extremely happy one. My grandfather, Yixizhongnai, was a scholarly man, versed in the Mongolian, Tibetan, and Chinese languages and especially good at painting and calligraphy. His large collection of Chinese paintings and calligraphies contributed to the development of my grandmother's embroidery art. A table plaque embroidered with natural scenery that she made at that time really represents the peak of her achievement. This piece of work, 133 centimetres long and about 100 centimetres wide, was embroidered with hills, streams, buildings, and human figures in color on a white ground—mountains rising one above the other, jagged rocks, clouds and streams dimly discernible, numerous figures in various postures—the larger ones are less than an inch in height, while the small ones appear like so many ants, yet all possessed of distinctive features. Although the work seemed, at first glance, to imitate the style of traditional Chinese landscape painting, it reminded one strongly of the great grasslands, for the red glaring sun, the wild geese flying high in the sky and the flocks of deer, sheep, and horses grazing in the valley were all embroidered with traditional Mongolian techniques. It is a

236. The late Ding Mongolian folk embroiderer Baoerjigude Cailajina.

pity that the work has now decayed. It can no longer be restored to its former splendor from the few fragments still in our possession.

The Mongolian people, being devout believers in Lamaism, regard the worship of Buddha as a major event in daily life. In our house, there was a special hall where we used to hold services in honor of Buddha and in which there were several pictures of Buddha embroidered by my grandmother along with the clay and wooden images. I was then only a small child and did not comprehend such things. But I still remember clearly what my grandmother told me about the hardships involved in embroidering a Buddha image. She must first of all undergo a period of fasting, then put up the embroidery frame in a quiet room, wash her hands, and burn incense. Before she began embroidering, she would draw the sketch with the extinguished incense stumps. Except for the prescribed rules as regards the image of Buddha to be embroidered, she was free to choose the designs and colors for the accompanying scenes and objects. This required a high level of skill and artistic taste. Each Buddha image would take her at least a couple of months to complete, and sometimes this could be as long as six months or one year. These products of her painstaking labor are treasures of our Mongolian embroidery art.

My grandfather died early, leaving my grandmother a widow in her middle age. Then she had the misfortune to lose my father, her only son. My brother and I were the only offspring who still lived with her. From then on, she was kept busy by housework and no longer took any interest in embroidery. These three images of Buddha are all that she has left behind her. Now, after a lapse of more than one hundred years, I can say with satisfaction that we have succeeded at last in preserving these embroideries in spite of difficulty. Before her death in 1949, my grandmother entrusted them to my wife, Shumin, who took good care of them despite the poverty of the family, so that they were kept in good condition. During the Cultural Revolution, our house was repeatedly ransacked. But my wife had them sewn into our clothes so that they were able to escape destruction. Moreover, the embroideries now appear just as fresh in color as when they were first made, even though they were often crumpled and wetted by perspiration in those years of trouble. It is indeed a great pleasure that we are able today to dedicate these precious specimens of Mongolian embroidery art to the public.

April, 1984
(Translated by Shi Huiqing)

158

237. An image of Zongkaba, the founder of new Lamaism, worked in the Mongolian style.

238, 239. Mongolian-style religious pictures.

Postscript

During my frequent participation in excavations of ancient relics, I often come upon exquisite pieces of folk embroidery. I am especially fond of the small functional articles, to the point of sometimes finding it difficult to part with them after I have finished studying them. These small embroideries were usually made by newly married women or girls reaching marriageable age, who expressed their feelings and longing for a happy life through their work. Primarily for decoration or gift-giving, these objects have remarkable workmanship and were cherished by their owners. This explains why they are so well preserved and we now have the chance to see them with our own eyes. The great quantities of embroidered relics excavated, worked in traditional folk designs with traditional folk stitching and shading techniques, provide ample opportunity for learning and help us form a general idea of the way in which Chinese folk embroidery progressed. I therefore dedicate this book — the result of my studies — to my teachers and those who share my interest. At the same time, I take delight in presenting readers with pictures of some of my favorite embroideries.

Ten years ago I was fortunate enough to be taught by Mr. Shen Congwen about ancient Chinese costumes and embroidery. I owe much to Mr. Congwen for his teaching and guidance. Despite his great age and poor health, Mr. Shen edited the Chinese edition of this book. I also want to thank Mr. Wang Xu for his valuable help. This book is a record of the results of their teaching expertise.

I should also like to express my gratitude to Mr. Zhang Zhenheng and Mr. Fu Xuiling for their support and assistance. Thanks are also due to Guangdong Provincial Museum, Zhongshan University at Guangzhou, Nanjing Museum, Hunan Provincial Museum, Jiangling Museum, Liaoning Provincial Museum, the Central Arts and Crafts Academy, Office of Historical Relics of Zhaowuda League of the Inner Mongolia Autonomous Region, Beijing Antique Shop, Mr. Li Keyu, Mr. Qi Congwen, and Mr. Suhe for their information and materials. Lastly, I extend my heartfelt thanks to the editors of the Commercial Press (Hong Kong), who have made possible the publication of this book.

May, 1987